There
Is
No
Death

The Extraordinary True Experience

of

Sarah LaNelle Menet

THERE IS NO DEATH

ISBN 0-9664970-5-8

First Edition 2002
Second Edition 2003
(Second Edition Notes: In the second edition, minor publishing errors were corrected. A
few additional details and personal life experiences were added along with some
photographs.)

3 4 5 6 7 8 9

Published by
Mountain Top Publishing
PO Box 97, Philipsburg, MT   59858
406-859-5555
www.thereisnodeath.com

Other related books and materials published by Mountain Top Publishing:

THERE IS NO DEATH AUDIO TAPE
(A live recording of a four-hour presentation by Sarah Menet,
including a question and answer session)

The Sequence of Events Leading to The Second Coming of Jesus Christ
By Roger K. Young
(A Christian guide listing and explaining the events that lead up to and include the Second
Coming of Jesus Christ, from the Old Testament to current times, showing how these events
relate to past and current events and the sequence in which they will happen. The guide
includes material from Sarah Menet's experience.)

ACKNOWLEDGMENTS

I sincerely want to express my love and appreciation to my Heavenly Father and His son Jesus Christ for the trials and triumphs I have experienced thus far while on the journey we call life. I am grateful to have been given an understanding of how we lived before we came to earth, why we are here, what the meaning of life is, and what waits for each of us when we leave this existence.

I am thankful for the wonderful and enlightened men and women who were lead by the Great God to assist in bringing this work to pass: Caren, Roger, Allan, and many others. I thank them for the endless hours of transcribing and editing, most of all for their personal efforts, support, and living examples of love to me. I pray that God will bless me with the light to draw my brothers and sisters throughout the world closer to Him who gave them life and loves each one of them.

TABLE OF CONTENTS

Chapter 7 *COMMONLY ASKED QUESTIONS AND ANSWERS*

INTRODUCTION

There is nothing new about near death experiences (NDEs). They have been happening since recorded history began. Sarah's experience is of great interest for several reasons, among which are the extensive detail and unusual scope of her visit to the world beyond and the way it relates to her life's story. She has emerged from her NDE and her incredibly difficult life as a strong and fervent voice for good conduct and a more noble and kind view of each other and our mortal experience. Her ability to influence minds and hearts toward a more enlightened and hopeful outlook has been life-changing to many distressed souls as well as to many who were searching for answers. If this book did no more than show that someone can go through all that Sarah has gone through and emerge victorious it would be completely worthy. But there is much more here, including warnings of impending difficulties.

Many people ask two questions concerning this book. When did she start telling people about her experience, including the events she saw in the future, and what religion or church did she belong to when she had the experience?

Sarah had her death experience in 1979 and for many years told only a few people. Then in 1988 when she almost died a second time, she felt strongly that she needed to tell more people of her experience, including the information of what she saw happening in the future.

Sarah is on video tape as early as 1995 talking about tall buildings in New York falling down, an economic collapse in the United States and around the world, a devastating biological attack on the United States, and other events.

At the time Sarah had her experience she was not a member of any organized religion. In fact, though raised as a Christian, she had come to be an agnostic. Believing that there probably was not a God, she therefore didn't care about religious questions or concerns.

It should be noted that even after her experience her life has not been easy. In 1996 she suddenly became blind because of her diabetes and a few days later collapsed from kidney failure and congestive heart failure. When she got out of the hospital, the doctors told her she needed to go onto dialysis immediately or she would probably die within a few months because her kidneys were only functioning at approximately one percent. She refused and unbelievably continues to constantly talk about her experience to all those who will listen. She spends a lot of time in the hospice program and also counsels often with those who have gone through or are going through tremendous trials of their own. She offers hope, compassion, and insight as she uniquely can. She keeps saying time is running out for our society faster than anyone can possibly understand.

Sarah says she looks forward to the time when she will be called back to the world of spirits she visited and be in the presence of her Savior one more time because she knows that there really is no such thing as death.

CHAPTER 1

My Life Before

I do not like the term near-death experience. There was nothing "near-death" about it, even though we refer to it as such. Those on the other side refer to it as the "new birth." Prior to the time when the paramedics pronounced me dead at the scene of my "successful" suicide, I had been seeking oblivion and darkness. Because of my horrific experiences in life, I had come to believe that there was no God and therefore, no afterlife. And so, when from somewhere near the ceiling I suddenly found myself watching the police and the paramedics work on my body, I learned that I had been quite wrong.

My story, however, cannot be told adequately without first giving a little background and history of my early life. I don't intend it to be a "pity me" story or a depressing one, even though that is exactly what it was for me for many, many years. It is necessary to take a glimpse into that part of my life in order to better understand the dramatic change that came into my heart as a result of my experience.

It needs to be said that before I attempted to take my life I was a completely miserable, unhappy, and bitter person, full of anger and hate. I hated people, I hated life, and I especially hated my life. The fact that such terrible things had happened merely proved to me that God did not exist, for if there were a God, He surely would not have allowed me to experience such pain, sorrow, and suffering. At the time, I actually hoped there was no life after death. That way I would not have to remember anything about my life. Life seemed to hold only unhappiness and misery and as such had lost all appeal for me.

These are the emotions that brought me to believe that the only alternative left for me was to end it all by taking my life. Though difficult to talk about even now, after so many years, I must describe the path I had traveled in life that ultimately led me to that day of despair.

MY LIFE BEFORE

While thinking about how to begin this book, I was sitting on the steps of my duplex looking up at the sky and had a flashback of when I was eight years old and there was a boy named Gregory in my neighborhood. He once told me that if you wished on the first star that appeared at night, there was great power there and your wish would surely come true. As a child I didn't have a lot of toys or pretty clothes, and there were a lot of possessions I could have wished for. However, later that night I found myself sitting on the steps of a run-down, red brick apartment in South Los Angeles, wishing that my father would die. This I did every night for as long as I could remember, because I truly hated my father.

As a little girl, I daydreamed a lot. For hours at a time I would sit on the couch or in the car and rock back and forth

2

and pretend that I was anywhere except where I was. Often in my imagination I was the princess being taken off to the dungeon by a wicked king or wizard or something like that. I would wait and wonder for long hours when "The Prince" was going to come and rescue me. He never did!

LaNelle (age 5) and Linda

When I was five I had a girlfriend named Linda that I played with quite a bit, not realizing that her mother actually was tending me. She lived just down the street from us, and her mother and mine were good friends. Linda had pretty clothes that were sewn for her and beautiful shiny hair ribbons and shoes to match. Her parents had purchased her a lovely piano to play, but she would whine and cry if she were asked to practice on it. I loved to sing and would perform for anyone. I told Linda that I would give anything to be able to play music, but she wouldn't allow me to touch the instrument. I felt sad that she had so much yet didn't seem to appreciate it and would gladly have traded places with her.

When not at Linda's house, I played with my cat, Mr. Midnight, the first of many pets. For most of my life I preferred animals to people. They were loyal, happy to see me, and beloved by me. They seemed to appreciate everything I did for them, and they never hurt me. During this time I also had a pet duck named Quack-Quack that followed me up and down the street everywhere I went. I was devastated when we returned home from a weekend trip to find him dead. Not long after that on an Easter egg hunt in our back yard, I also found my Mr. Midnight dead under our house. Shortly thereafter we moved again, and I found myself alone without anything to love.

At any given time I would bring another "critter" home to love, but one by one like Quack-Quack and Mr. Midnight they all disappeared. I often wondered why every time I loved something, it was always taken away from me. (I learned as an adult that our mother would have someone take them to be abandoned because we couldn't afford to feed them.)

A LIVING HELL

Growing up in Los Angeles for me is perhaps described best as a living hell, a nightmare that never seemed to end—a bad dream that would continually get worse. My father was most often the creator of our nightmares. I did not know as a child that my father had been a pedophile and a child molester. We had all grown up with his violent temper. My brother Don and oldest sister Sandra (from Mother's first marriage) left home at a very early age because of the abuse. Don ran away at the age of nine and Sandra was taken out of the home around the age of three.

Whippings were too frequently a part of our childhood. These were not spankings, but they were harsh punishments where we were often hit with inappropriate objects. One of these was called a blackjack. It was a thick leather strap with heavy metal encased in the ends; it had been used in years past as a police weapon. I will describe just a few instances of this abuse as I tell my story.

My father could lose control almost at any time towards any member of the family. On one occasion, at the age of eight and while we were still living in the red brick apartment, I stayed home from school one day, not feeling well, and awoke to the sounds of a struggle. Walking into the front room, I found my father trying to choke my mother to death. He would surely have done so if I had not come into the room. He was unaware of my presence in the house, and the shock of seeing me stopped him and, I believe, ultimately saved her life. That was the first time I remember being awakened during the night by people who took me away to stay at their home for a short while.

THERE IS NO GOD

At this same time, events started taking place that convinced me that God could not exist, or if he did he did not care about me or ever hear my prayers. The age of eight seemed to be an important period in my life when particular belief patterns developed. A formative event occurred then that left a heavy impression on me.

My mother had a dear friend who was the most beautiful woman I had ever seen. Even as a small child I was impressed with her beauty. She had raven black hair and dancing eyes. I can remember thinking how happy she was. In my child's mind she looked like a grown-up version of Snow White from the fairy tale. One day when I came home from

5

Father, Mother, Linda, Deborah and LaNelle

school, I found my mother crying. Even though I had seen her crying like this many times, it still disturbed me. I asked her what was wrong. She explained that her best friend Sheryl might be dying. Mother took me into her bedroom, and we knelt beside the bed where we prayed for her dear friend. Mother said that if our faith were strong enough, Sheryl would be healed and made well. She had taught me about God and prayer, so I prayed with all the faith I could. I wanted this wonderful request to be answered. As a child does, even in difficult circumstances, I resumed the business of play and left behind all cares and fears.

A few days later, mother was very distraught. She told me that Sheryl had passed away. I was shocked at the news of her death. I was so sure that our fervent prayer on behalf of this beautiful woman would help her recover. My mother, being deeply depressed over the loss of her best friend, did not take the time to explain to a young child that the Lord's will, what He knows best, was also a factor in prayers such as ours.

Sometimes it is just a person's time to go. In my mind I just could not understand why Sheryl had died, and I was very hurt that our prayer had not "worked," as my mother said it would. We attended the funeral a few days later. There was a long procession to her coffin, and I spent the time thinking that when I got up there I was going to ask God to restore her life. Everything is so simple in the mind of a child. So, as we approached the coffin, I asked my mother to lift me up so I could kiss Sheryl goodbye. As she did, I said, "Please God, let my mother's friend come back to life and be well." But Sheryl did not move. She was still and silent. I wanted to say that I knew God could restore her life; but the line was long, and we had to move on.

As the reality of the moment hit me, and we watched the coffin lowered into the ground, I thought that maybe my mother was wrong. Maybe there is no God. If there were an all powerful God who cared about us like my mother said, wouldn't he have brought this beautiful woman back to life? So between my father, our home life, and this first experience with death and my confusion regarding it, I came to the conclusion that God could not, in fact did not, exist. Subsequent events seemed only to confirm this conclusion.

As years passed, circumstances did not improve. When I was ten years old, my family was sitting on an old brown couch eating ice cream. My mother asked me to pass her a pillow. As I did, the pillow hit the tip of my spoon and flicked a few drops of ice cream onto the couch. I hadn't noticed it, but my father stood up, yelled at me, and started hitting me repeatedly on my head and eventually knocked me unconscious. I didn't even know what had happened until hours later. I awoke to the sound of my mother standing over me crying. My father was there also. This was the only time he showed any remorse. He repeated over and over again, "I am sorry." The words had little meaning for me. True remorse meant that it wouldn't happen again, but of course I knew it would. Soon after this happened, my parents separated again. We moved to a white apartment on National Boulevard in West Los Angeles.

POOR HEALTH

Along with the abuse, my health was very poor, which did not help matters much. One day while walking home through the Presbyterian Church yard from the elementary school around the corner, I collapsed. I woke up some time later in the hospital and was not happy to see my mother and father both there. The doctor's evaluation was that I was suffering from malnutrition—I weighed only 60 pounds. I had been living mostly on cheap white bread and mayonnaise and for some odd reason drank a lot of diluted vinegar water. Because of this ordeal, my parents moved to another apartment on Sepulveda a few blocks away and next to the freeway. In the front room of this typical Los Angeles apartment, my parents remarried for the third time.

Not long after we moved there, I had been outside talking with the next-door neighbor boy, John, when my father yelled out for me to come into the house. I replied, "Just a minute," and went on talking for only a few minutes. When I came into the apartment, my father was furious that I had not come in immediately when he called me. He removed his thin leather belt and repeatedly whipped me with it on my back. Small streaks of blood came through my little white blouse. He sent me to my room and ordered me to stay there, and he and my mother continued in a serious argument. When they left, I was determined to run away from home and went to Lynn's house. She was a girlfriend I knew from school. I told both her and her mother what had happened. When her mother expressed a desire to notify the police, I became afraid of her making the situation worse, so I ran back home as fast as I could and stayed in my room until my parents returned.

While we were there my sister Linda married a wonderful young man in the Air Force. His name was John, and they moved far away. I hadn't spent a lot of time with her prior to this because of the age difference. My oldest sister Sandra, who had been gone from home for a long time, came and packed up my clothes and moved me to Long Beach to live with her, her husband, and baby daughter Julie. Sandra was wonderful and I loved her, but she prepared food I wasn't used to eating. When I ate the fresh fruit she gave me, my mouth broke out in painful blisters. My system wasn't used to that. I gave her a hard time over the food she prepared. She kept a clean and tidy apartment, but I was always afraid about living so close to the ocean—only one-half block away. At night I could hear the waves crashing and I was terrified. I stayed with Sandra for a year until she had her second child Carl and then returned home again.

A STRANGE RELATIONSHIP

The relationship between my mother and father was anything but normal. They were actually married and divorced on three different occasions—and separated dozens of times. He was cheating on my mother long before I was born and was continuing to do so at the time of my birth. In fact, he insisted on naming me after one of his girlfriends named Nell. Mother changed it to LaNelle.

For years my mother tried to escape from him. She took us away a hundred times it seemed, but he would always return. He would threaten to kill her or us if she didn't go back to him. Once, in his rage, my father drove our car with Mom and I in it to the edge of a cliff in the Santa Susana Pass in Simi Valley and threatened to drive the car over the edge. He had one foot on the break and the other pressing on the gas pedal revving up the engine, all the while cursing and screaming. Mom and I cried and pleaded with him not to do it. As adults we learned that he had done this same horrible act alone with her in the past. After that traumatic night, I was too afraid to ever make a move or express how I felt about anything.

ALWAYS MOVING

Another unbearable stress in my childhood was our constant moving. We never lived in one place for very long. I can remember at the age of 18 trying to count how many places we had lived. When I reached about 50, I gave up. Much of the moving was my mother trying to get us away, to escape our father's violence and his criminal activity with children in the neighborhoods where we lived. It was difficult to maintain lasting friendships or build meaningful memories from any one particular place. My schooling was hit-and-miss because of the frequent relocating. In my last year of high school, I attended five different schools within a 12-month period. I never did get a diploma because my parents pulled me out of a temporary home four months before I would have graduated.

In addition to the constant moving throughout the years, I lived with seven different "foster" families. I was not accepted well and a few times was called a "rag doll" or "white trash" because of my used clothing. The feeling of being shuffled around, misplaced, and just worthless was always with me. I never really felt like I belonged to anything or anyone and was very unhappy. These homes were not government sponsored, subsidized, or inspected, but places arranged through friends or church members. Only one of these homes provided any real happiness. When I think back to a place I call home, it would be that beautiful house on Ocean View Avenue in Mar Vista, California, with the Klingman family and their daughter Joanne.

JOANNE

I met Joanne around the age of 12 and we became best friends instantly. She was beautiful, came from a somewhat prominent family, a very structured lifestyle, and lived in a very nice house. She had a brother named Richard and three older sisters: Pat, Barbara, and Diane. Her mother cooked health foods, and after living with them for one month, I gained 18 pounds. I felt happy and secure there. Joanne and I shared a bedroom and did everything together. We had fun doing what we called taking "Pot Shots." We made it a game to take unusual pictures like digging in a trash can pretending to look for food or finding someone's very fancy car and sitting on it like it was ours. We were very creative at times. She introduced me to new foods like yogurt, which I had never heard of before.

Even though I felt safe and secure and Joanne and I had a lot of fun, there was an underlying problem in the house. Apparently it was the father's idea to take me in and care for me,

My sister Joanne

not the mother's. She felt that I wasn't good enough to be around her daughter and expressed it openly. It caused many fights between "Jo-Jo" and her mom because my new "sister" was always defending me. Her mother entered our room once when I was alone and said if it weren't for the kindness of her husband I would not be in their home. The day before a couple of nice boys had come from school to visit me and Joanne. Her mother let me know that boys like that would not be interested in a girl like me. Once again, I felt unworthy for anything good in my life. Soon the two sisters, Barbara and Diane, were going to have a double wedding and I was told that there was too much going on for me to stay in their home any longer. From there I went to live with the Cliffords in Santa Monica, then with the Chewnings in Simi Valley, and finally with the Scott family.

Between times of living with these families, my mother and I moved twice back and forth out of California. When I was 18, Mother informed me that she and my father were divorcing again. She wanted to move far away from LA and she wanted me to go with her, but I refused. That is when I moved in with the Scott family. Mrs. Scott helped me learn a lot about housecleaning, cooking, and doing laundry. They were very nice to me, but I still had the same old feeling that I didn't have a home and was really all alone in the world.

MY FIRST MARRIAGE

While living with them, I met a young boy by the name of Mike. He seemed to be part of a "real" family. They had seven children and a large, immaculate home. His mother was gentle and kind and represented the role of a mother who could accomplish anything. I really fell in love with his family. They had moved to Simi Valley when I was living with the Scott's. Mike was blonde, handsome, a snow skier, and rode a Triumph 650 motorcycle. He wore nice clothes and was very popular at church and school. All this was intriguing to me. I was amazed that he wanted me for a girlfriend, so we began a relationship. I became pregnant, and his father, who was a clergyman, married us in their beautiful home. Because I had no idea what real love was and desired to escape my past, we pretty much had a nonphysical marriage relationship. I knew it was my fault, and because of my coldness toward my young husband, he was driven to find love elsewhere. My escape was short-lived. After three short years and the birth of two sons, Sean and Chad, we were divorced.

MY FATHER DIES

During my marriage to Mike and just before the birth of my first child Sean, word came that my father was dying of cancer. I don't think I had ever been happier about anything in my life. Even though I was fairly sure that God did not exist, I found myself thanking him that this man was dying. The torture was finally going to be over. Our mother and the rest of us would be free of him at last. However, he asked mother if she would care for him in her home. She agreed, and I could hardly believe it.

There Is No Death

When my father reached the point where he was so ill that he could no longer care for himself or even move, I went to the hospital to visit him. What a sight! Imagine a man of six feet two inches weighing approximately 70 pounds. Finally, I was the one in control of the situation. He couldn't hurt me anymore, so it was safe to tell him just how I felt. I was vicious. I said every vile, nasty, mean, and evil thing I could think of. I told him that I hated him and that I hoped he burned in Hell for everything he had done to me and to my family. I was glad he was in pain. I let all of the hate pour out of me, and I told him that he was responsible for my horrible childhood and the reason I could not function as an adult. I blamed him for every mistake I had ever made.

To my utter astonishment, in the middle of my tirade, he held out his arms and asked me to forgive him. What a nerve he had! I said, "I hate you and am so glad that you are dying. I am glad that you are in pain and I will never visit your grave. I would spit on your grave." I left the hospital room angry but with some satisfaction that finally I had been able to say all of the things I had felt for so long. About a week later he died. My sister Deborah attended the funeral to support our mother, but my brother and other sisters and I didn't go. I didn't shed a tear. That part of the nightmare was over. Now, I thought, maybe I could make something of my life.

After my divorce I did whatever I could to care for my children. I took jobs that were available to an uneducated, single mom. I cleaned houses, waited tables, and did ironing at ten cents per piece. I would iron 40 garments a day and earn just $4. I found myself moving my children from place to place because of circumstances and eventually gained a better understanding of my mother's "mistakes." A few times I entered

14

into relationships just so I could better care for the children, but it always ended in disaster for everyone involved.

HEALTH PROBLEMS RETURN

Shortly before the end of my marriage to Mike, my health began to fail. I started having headaches, constant thirst, and never-ending exhaustion. As a child I was always frail and did not have much strength. My poor health was aggravated partly, I am sure, by the mistreatment from my father. No doubt the stress, abuse, and poor nutrition I received as a child contributed to the health problems I started to experience as an adult.

So, at 21 years old, I was diagnosed with Type 1 diabetes, and I learned that I would have to take insulin shots every day to control it. I had always been terrified of needles and injections. A few times in the past I had to have shots for various reasons, immunizations, and a blood test required for a marriage license. I needed to lie down so that I wouldn't faint when I saw the needle. To be told that I had to take shots every day for the rest of my life was more than I could accept—I said I would rather die. Once more life had knocked me down with a crushing blow.

I MARRY "MY FATHER"

At the age of 22, I remarried. This time it was to a young man who everyone referred to as the "golden boy." He was very handsome and had been the most popular guy in high school. He was class president and star of the football team. Also, he was brilliant. I had known him since I was 14 years old but ran into him again in Salt Lake City during a

*Chad, Sean and Glenn (front)
about 1975*

meeting at the University of Utah. He was attending medical school there. This time I married because I really was in love. I remember commenting to my family that I couldn't believe someone like him would want to marry me.

After one week into our marriage, I made a phone call to my former mother-in-law, whom I still loved very much, asking her for a recipe. When he discovered who I was talking to, he grabbed the phone, hung it up, and slapped my face. He told me that I was never to call anyone from that family again. I soon discovered that I had put myself into a situation very much resembling my earlier years. My new husband, Glenn, had a violent temper also. He began physically abusing me as well as my two sons, Sean and Chad, from my previous marriage. He would often whip them with his belt. On one occasion he beat Chad with a wire hanger for getting into my makeup. Sometimes he would punish them for imagined misbehaviors by not allowing them to go to the bathroom. He would make them hold their urine for as long as they could. When the boys finally wet their pants, he would whip them and drag them out into the yard where he would hose them down.

This was the worst of all possible nightmares. I had married "my father" and now my children were being abused as I had been.

I made excuses for the abuse as "stress" because he was a medical student and had a lot of pressures. It had to have been hard to marry a girl with two children, attend school, and work two jobs. I now realize that there was much more to it than that. He was also a product of his environment and upbringing, just as I was.

During our three-year marriage we were separated 11 times. To make matters more complicated, we brought a third child into the world. Again, more than ever, my life was in turmoil, and I had nowhere to turn. Each time we separated, I was left with no money and all the children to care for. I moved where I could, sometimes out of state to stay with friends or family. After he committed adultery, our marriage ended in a bitter divorce. I wanted out so badly that I didn't contest anything and left with just the children and our clothes. I was on the edge of a nervous breakdown worrying about Glenn, who was livid about losing custody of the son we had together.

Years later, before Glenn's death, he confessed that his mistreatment of my sons and me was motivated by insane jealousy. The thought of the relationship with another man that had resulted in the birth of these two beautiful blonde boys was more than he could handle. In his mind he could never be second. We also discovered that a second party had plotted to destroy our marriage and had succeeded. I learned that open communication is vital to any relationship, and things are not always as they appear. We were able to forgive the mistakes of the past and became friends shortly before he died.

17

I went back to doing the same type of work I had done previously. Soon I discovered that because of my hard work and the fact that men found me attractive, I was able to find work serving at parties for wealthy people in Beverly Hills and Bel Air. The money was better than what I had been able to make previously. I have to admit that there was also a certain excitement involved in attending the parties, even if it was in the capacity of a servant. I was presently living in Beverly Hills on Doheny Drive in a one-room single apartment that had a Murphy bed that folded up into the wall. I was still depressed, angry, and having trouble taking care of my children and myself. At times I found it hard to even feed the children if work was scarce and I had no one to turn to. Once for an entire week all four of us had only one bag of potatoes to eat.

Christmas Eve came and I had nothing for the boys. The pain of our situation was almost too great for me to bear. I cried and told the boys how sorry I was that I had nothing for them. They were so sweet and said that it was all right. They understood and didn't need anything. That made me feel even worse. What kind of a mother was I? We were living in a one-room bachelor apartment with no food to eat and no hope for Christmas. A knock came at the door. It was Joanne. She brought in a tree with decorations and a few sacks of groceries and presents for everyone. What had I done to deserve her in my life? Nothing, I thought. I didn't trust anyone, and I mocked and ridiculed everything in a desperate attempt to make some sense out of a life that was completely out of control.

Eventually a few jobs serving at parties evolved into a household cook position for a prominent family in Beverly Hills. I had worked hard during the last few years, earning a reputation for gourmet cooking, decorating, and organizing

18

large estates. This eventually landed me jobs working for several well-known celebrities. During the day I would work in these mansions, and at night I would serve at parties surrounded by glamorous people. A wonderful girl named Anita, who managed the apartment building where I lived, would watch my children for me at night. My plan was to somehow save my money and get out of Los Angeles. Too much had happened there for me to stay any longer. It carried too many dark memories. And then the black cloud that seemed ever-present in my life grew darker still.

THE "PROPOSITION"

The owner of this single apartment building was a well-to-do foreigner. He knew that I was struggling and didn't have much money. One night, after I served for a party at his home, he approached me with a proposition: free rent, a decorated apartment, and certain other privileges if I would just be "friendly" to his brother who had seen me at the party. Well, I knew that being friendly meant sleeping with him, and even though I was a dysfunctional person, I did not do things like that. When I turned down my landlord's "generous" offer, he began threatening me. I couldn't believe things could turn on me so quickly and completely, but it seemed to be the story of my life. Just when I began to look up, I was knocked down again.

My landlord continued to pressure me and threaten to have me killed if I didn't give in. I became more depressed and desperate. As my problems came to a head in a moment of complete despair, I sat on the front porch of my apartment and cried openly, trying to think of how I was going to get out of this mess.

I must have presented quite a picture with my head buried in my arms and sobbing, because while I was sitting there, as if in the script of a movie, a big limousine pulled up. A man got out and asked, "Are you okay?" I broke down and told him the whole story. He told me he was a Hollywood producer and had a very large estate in Bel Air on San Ysidro Drive. He and his lady friend had a baby, and he would pay me $2,500 a month to live in their home, cook for them, and care for the infant.

Maybe there is a God, I thought. One month's salary would be all I needed to get out of Los Angeles and find some peace and a safer place for my sons. One catch was that I could not bring my children with me to the new job. I decided to accept the offer. Even though sending the boys away would be a tremendous sacrifice, I felt that it would only be temporary, just until I had earned enough money to relocate and start over.

By this time Mike, the two older boys' father, had remarried, and he and his new wife welcomed the chance to have Sean and Chad stay with them for a while. My youngest son, then seven years old, went to live with a kind clergyman and his family in West Los Angeles. With all of the boys placed safely in good homes, I was free to take the job that I hoped would lead to a new start for all of us. All I wanted to do was get out of Los Angeles and California.

As could easily be imagined from the way things had been going in the past, it soon became apparent that all was not as it seemed to be in the new job. Yes, this man was indeed a producer, but after I moved in I found out that he was also one of the largest cocaine dealers in Hollywood. I learned that at one time he had been a talented movie producer but had decided that the easy way to make more money was by dealing drugs. Movie stars and other "Hollywood people" came to the house at all hours of the day and night. Most often they would disappear into the producer's bedroom with him and emerge a short time later and leave.

My suspicions were confirmed at a huge party he threw as Hollywood celebrities partook of the white powder he had placed in containers around the room. It was cocaine, but I didn't care—that is, until one night not long after the party. I was alone in the house with their baby and talking with my "sister" Joanne on the phone about what I was going to do. I hadn't been paid yet. He was always coming up with excuses saying, "In a few more days I'll have more money."

All of a sudden I heard someone pick up the receiver on another phone in the house, and I asked, "Who is this, who's in the house?" The voice on the other end said, "Hang up or we'll cut your throat." I was terrified and ran out of the house, making my way to a few of the neighbor's homes, banging on their doors and screaming hysterically that someone had broken into the house. We had to save the baby who was left alone there.

Either no one was home, they were all too afraid to get involved, or they just didn't care. Regardless, no doors were opened to me that night. Finally a van drove by. I flagged it down and quickly explained the situation. They drove off and called the police. The officers arrived in minutes in cars and helicopters and caught the men who had entered the house—druggies looking for cocaine. The police also arrested the producer when he arrived home because of the drugs they discovered. I hadn't lived there even six weeks and now this disaster. Without a paycheck, what was I going to do?

Of course I had to leave—with no money and nowhere to go. This was the last straw. I was convinced that nothing I could do would ever work out, and all was hopeless. Then Shaun, a movie editor with whom I had become acquainted, offered to let me stay at his place. He was a friend and "customer" of the producer. He had been kind, and somehow I felt I could trust him when he offered me a safe place to stay temporarily. Besides, I had nowhere else to go.

While living in Shaun's apartment, I tried to help out by keeping the place clean. Our relationship was one of friends. He had bailed me out of a tough situation, so I thought I could help him in some way. A few days later while cleaning up, I discovered a stash of cocaine. I was shocked and upset because I believed he was a "normal" guy. Out of anger I flushed the entire bag down the toilet. When he came home that day I confronted him with my discovery and told him what I had done with it. Upon finding that thousands of dollars worth of cocaine had gone down the drain, he was furious. We argued and he left. When he didn't come back after four days, I finally called the studio where he worked. The person answering the phone told me that Shaun had locked himself in the editing room, and no one had seen him for the entire time. I was concerned and upset and drove down to the studio. I knocked on the door and when he wouldn't answer, threatened to call the police if he didn't open up. When he did, it was a sad sight to see him with huge dark circles under his eyes. He was shaking and obviously on a binge. All he said was, "Leave me alone," and then he closed the door.

It didn't matter what I did, my life was a total failure. I was so depressed I wasn't even in control of what I was doing. I was walking around in a daze. I went back to Shaun's apartment, and all the mistakes and failures of the past ran through my mind. I began to cry and put a 45-rpm record on the record player that I had set to play over and over again. It kept repeating the words, "Do it or die." I listened to the words and decided I was never going to "do it" or anything else of any worth and decided I should die.

THE SUICIDE

On that fateful day, I couldn't go on any longer. I hated people even more than I did before, and just breathing in and out was painful. I couldn't get rid of the thought that my children deserved better than what I could give them. I couldn't even take care of myself! I was useless, and it would be best for everyone if I just went away. All I ever dreamed of was to find my knight in shining armor and have a little family and live happily ever after.

I had sprained my ankle a few months earlier roller-skating, and the doctor had given me a prescription of pain pills. I was very much into health foods and hated drugs so had placed the medication on the shelf unopened. That day I took the entire bottle of Tylenol with codeine and may have taken a few other things with it—I don't remember.

Apparently, as I was losing consciousness, I called my sister Deborah who had moved to Utah. Later she told me that I asked her to tell our mother that I loved her and that I forgave her. Subconsciously I must have felt that she should have done more to protect us from our father, although now I know that she did everything she was capable of. With that said, I collapsed. Because of my slurred speech, the things I said, and me not answering anymore, my sister knew something was very wrong and called the Los Angeles police department. By the time they reached the apartment building, I was out of my body and looking down on everything from somewhere near the ceiling.

I could see the police as they knocked on the door to the building. A neighbor let them in. They came to the door of the apartment where I was and knocked and yelled. When no one answered, one of them kicked the door open. I watched as the police and two paramedics came rushing into the room where I was lying on the floor. They started taking vitals, and one of them said, "No heartbeat, no pulse—she's dead." While this was happening I was watching it all from above the room. My body was very pale and my lips were blue. It was strange, but I didn't think of the body I could see as me, or even a part of me. It was just a clump of clay.

I listened to their conversations and watched them quickly walk from room to room. At that point they had not yet determined what had happened. One policeman went into the bedroom and was looking around. Another walked into the bathroom and started going through the medicine cabinet. Under the sink he found my medical bag and my insulin. He yelled out, "I think she might be a diabetic," and continued looking through everything under the sink. While he was doing this, one of the paramedics took the phone out of my hand and hung it up. It rang almost immediately. The paramedic picked it up and asked, "Do you have any information on this girl that is here? We found a dead body."

When he said this, I thought it was very strange. I was not dead. I could hear and see everything perfectly. I could also hear through the wire and heard the man who had called say he didn't know anything. I find it strange and wonderful that while all of this was happening, I was able to see everything all at the same time, regardless of where it took place. Walls of brick or wood did not seem to hinder my vision at all. At that time it all seemed very natural. I was mesmerized by all of the activity that somehow, in some removed, distant way, had to do with me.

While one paramedic was talking on the phone, the other was still working on me. When the one hung up the receiver, the other said, "She hasn't been gone for long. Her body is still warm. Let's try to revive her. Get the paddles out." All this interaction took place within a moment of time. When they said this, I became upset and tried talking to them. I said, "Leave it alone." I did not want to go back into that clump of clay. I think I said it twice, and then when they ignored me, I lost interest. Instantly, I was no longer floating in the air above them. I was standing at the edge of a beautiful silver lake.

CHAPTER 2

THE WORLD OF SPIRITS
"Beautiful Beyond Description"

THE SILVER LAKE

The move from the previous location was instantaneous. In less than a blink of an eye I found myself in an entirely different world from the one I had inhabited since birth—a world unlike anything I had ever seen or imagined. In the distance and all around me were magnificent hills covered with trees, grass, and flowers of every hue imaginable. I stood by a large and beautiful lake located to the right of me and I felt no fear, which was very unusual.

So that the significance of this can be understood, I need to explain that everyone who knows me can verify that I have an intense, almost irrational fear of water. I cannot swim a stroke and am horrified of the possibility of drowning. When I was younger, on the only family vacation

27

that I can remember, my father decided that he would cure me of my phobia of water and teach me to swim all at the same time. He pushed me into the lake. I swallowed water, panicked, and felt as if I were going to drown. The result of my father's actions was only to succeed in making the situation worse. Ever since then I have been unable to walk around the deep end of a swimming pool because I have been deathly afraid of accidentally falling in. It's only within these last few years that I've been able to get into a hot tub without being overcome with anxiety. When I say that I was standing beside a lake without any fear whatsoever, it is extremely significant.

Now, as I stood before this very large lake, the intense fear that had always been a part of me was inexplicably gone. Fear was replaced with a fascination for the body of water that spread out next to me. It was overwhelmingly beautiful. The water glistened like diamonds and had the appearance of liquid silver. As I leaned over the edge, the water was crystal clear, and I found that I could see for miles, clear down to the bottom. I don't know how deep it was, but it was very, very deep. There were tremendous numbers and varieties of fish swimming through the underwater foliage that was everywhere waving in the currents. The fish and the foliage were of the most vivid colors—very bright and not of our world.

The only way to describe the colors I saw there would be to explain that the spectrum as we know it in this world is muted and dulled, as though seen through some sort of glass that makes colors subdued and somehow less vibrant. To state that our vision in this life is vastly limited would be an understatement. Here we are able to see only a tiny fraction of what I could see there. Not only are the colors like nothing we can imagine, but the words do not exist in our vocabulary to adequately describe them.

As I stood at the edge of this magnificently beautiful shimmering lake, I was enticed by the water and wanted to fall into it and allow it to surround or envelop me. Instinctively I knew that the water was alive in its own way with a spirit about itself, and that it would not harm me. I wasn't aware of how this knowledge came to me, just that it did. The curiosity lasted only for a moment, and then my attention turned to the rest of my surroundings.

BEAUTIFUL SURROUNDINGS

I looked up away from the water to the setting surrounding the lake. It was simply breathtaking. Everywhere there were wonderful flowers and vegetation unknown to our world. The flowers were so different in color and so vibrant that I can still see them clearly in my mind today but again cannot begin to describe them. I have no names for them and to try and describe the colors would be like explaining red or blue to a person blind from birth.

The grass was a bright, vivid green and felt like soft, lush velvet. There was a gentle warm breeze that caused ripple patterns in the grass. The trees were of various shades and their branches moved similar to the swaying grass. Never in my life have I seen anything in nature to match the beauty of what I saw in that realm.

My attention turned from what I could take in around me to how well I could see. I noticed my eyesight was

29

enhanced and so sharp that I could literally see for miles. When I stood looking at something in the distance, concentrating on an object, it would appear to grow closer and closer, somewhat like the function of a telephoto lens. In a moment I could see what I was focusing on as if I were standing right next to it. There was nothing I could not look at or see. Distance was not a deterrent, and the area was expansive. I was fascinated by this new ability and just stood there for some time looking around.

While still beside the lake, I made another discovery. As I turned my head slowly to the left to take in the view, I saw in the distance a beautiful hill blanketed with trees. I thought how much I would like to go in that direction and be there. No sooner did I think this thought than I began moving toward the hill. It was almost as though the movement was initiated by the beginning of my thought. It was wonderful and I was there in a second. It was all so smooth and happened so quickly that before I realized it I stood at the top of the hill. It was even more beautiful up close than it had been from a distance. Several large groups of lovely, bright green trees swayed softly in the gentle breeze. They looked a little like weeping willows and their branches almost touched the grass around them as they moved.

The sky was a wonderful deep rich blue and there were objects floating in it which at first appeared to be clouds. As I looked closer, I could see that they were actually formations of swirling light with a cloudlike appearance. It was unusual and breathtaking, yet it felt perfectly normal.

As I looked around, drinking it all in, a tremendous feeling of peace came over me. Here I was, separated from everything that I had known before and there were no feelings of loss for the possessions I had left behind. My material treasures, my dear children, or anyone else that might have loved me were not on my mind. All I could think of was how very wonderful it was to be in this place.

My newly acquired senses soon made me aware that the grove of trees I stood in and the plants and grass around me were alive and communicating to me that they not only knew who I was but were happy that I was there with them. While not thinking like we do, they nonetheless seemed to have feelings and a form of intelligence that, though different from our own, was still very real. I stood there for a while feeling the love for me that radiated from these forms of life that I now viewed from a completely different perspective. It was then that I started to ask, or rather think of, questions about this new world that I had come into. The questions started with Where am I? and quickly went on from there.

QUESTIONS AND ANSWERS

As this question and answer period started, I noticed something very different about my mind. It was not the same as it had been on earth. Our mortal thoughts are pretty well limited to one thought at a time. But while I stood in this remarkable world, I could and did ask what seemed like hundreds of questions at the same time. Not only that, but the answers came back to me instantly, and I comprehended them all perfectly. I continued to ask more and more questions. I was amazed at the capabilities of my spirit-mind and so stood there for several moments just asking questions and receiving the answers. Later, as I looked around making observations regarding my surroundings, answers to thoughts and questions flooded my mind instantaneously in the same way.

During this period of enlightenment, which seemed to continue for quite a while, I learned that time did not exist there as we think of it on earth. Again, I must say that this is all very difficult to explain with our limited vocabulary to those who have not experienced it. Suffice it to say that in this spirit world there are no seconds, minutes, hours, or days. There are no nights either, and the limitations of time as we know it just do not exist. Time itself seemed to be able to change by going slower or much faster. The restrictions that are on earth with regard to vision, hearing, and smelling simply do not exist there. In fact, there is complete freedom of thought, vision, and all the senses, as far as I could tell, with time included. The spirit world has similarities at first glance, but closer inspection revealed obvious differences.

Regarding the sense of smell, there is a fragrance that exists there which is incredible and unlike anything earthly that I have ever smelled before. This scent is not like any perfume, spice, or earthly flower. If I concentrate, I can still remember it clearly. It made me feel peaceful, restful, and calm. This fragrance made me feel alive and wonderful, just as everything else did. Every sense is accentuated and contributes to the feeling of well-being that permeates that amazing world, like being wrapped in a blanket of love.

THE DREAM COTTAGE

As I stood on the hill asking questions and receiving answers, I paused to look at something that caught my interest off in the distance. It was a lovely little cottage in a meadow far away. It seemed so serene and perfect. Situated in an area surrounded with trees, flowers, and little streams, it appeared like a little cottage out of a fairytale book. It had a round-topped door, a cobblestone path leading up to it, and what appeared to be a soft thatched roof. On taking a closer look I realized that it was not as I first assumed and that the cottage was actually very large.

While gazing upon this idyllic scene I thought, I would love to live in such a house. Immediately the answer came: You can. You can live in whatever type of building or house that would make you happy. At the same time I understood that I could live in a simple cottage like this one or in a columned mansion with family and friends. The decision regarding our living circumstances is primarily up to us, although within the limits of what we have earned.

ANIMALS IN THE SPIRIT WORLD

As I looked at the cottage and admired how pretty and perfect it was, I noticed a dog trotting along a path. The dog appeared to be like an Irish setter with long brown hair. I was somewhat surprised and thought to myself, Are there pets here? The response that filled my mind was that there are animals here of all kinds, some of which have been pets to people on earth. I was given to understand that if a person had pets they loved and cared for in mortality and if the animals also loved them and wanted to be with them, they could then be together forever.

As I looked at the dog, it seemed to sense my presence and looked back at me. I could hear and feel its thoughts of recognition. This surprised me a little. Then immediately I understood that the spirits of animals and people could communicate and understand each other the same way I had

33

communicated with the plants earlier, that is, telepathically. The difference being that the animals communicated on a higher level than the trees and grass but still well below the level of my thoughts.

It also came to my mind that on earth the animals could understand people but that our ability to understand them had been taken away. The thoughts of animals are simple, like the thoughts of a child, and they have personalities, feelings, and desires as well. One of the reasons that animals exist on earth is to help us learn to love. There are some individuals who have not developed the ability to love other people but are capable of loving animals. I also understood that the spirits of animals are precious, and those who take their lives without cause or are cruel to them will have serious consequences to pay.

THE CITY OF LIGHT

My attention turned to the view miles away. I saw what appeared to be numerous cities filled with magnificent buildings and many people. The cities seemed to glow in the distance like brilliant light was coming from them. Then I realized that the scene did not include many separate cities but was only one enormous city filled with spirit beings. Though miles away, I was again able to use my unlimited vision and see it as though I were standing in front if it.

As I remained on the top of the hill surveying the city before me, I became aware that I was not clothed. I was completely naked, and yet my state of undress did not concern me in the least. I had no thoughts of being seen by others, even though I could see that there were thousands down below in the city. When I thought about clothing, I immediately understood that I had not passed through the barrier or "film" that separates this spirit world from the mortal world. If I had, a loved one would have greeted me and brought me garments to put on. The "film" is like a thin transparent wall of some fine matter that, by passing through it, prevents one from going back to earth life.

I also understood that whenever anyone passes from mortality, no matter what their status or behavior on earth, they are greeted by a loved-one almost instantly and given a robe to wear. The clothing given identifies the wearer as a new arrival and is called a "new-spirit-entrant robe." These robes differ from the ones worn by other spirits that have been in the spirit world for a longer time. In that way, when a new arrival is greeted, they are recognized and received with a warm welcome. The robes worn by others also identified the wearers as having some authority or gave an indication of the responsibilities they had. I understood that there was great order in everything that was performed there and that the assignments or responsibilities of an individual were those a person chose or had agreed to. Some were asked to perform certain tasks, but the choice was always theirs to do it or not. Everything was voluntary and there was never any force.

As I looked further at the city of light, I noticed that there were streets and paths all lined with flowers and shrubs. Lovely fountains were present that sprayed the silvery water I had seen earlier at the lake. As the water sprayed into the air it appeared like a million sparkling diamonds full of life and energy too beautiful to describe with words. There were people walking everywhere, though there was not any feeling of hurrying. It was very calm and peaceful and relaxed. There were also small groups of people standing and sitting on the grass in the parklike areas between the buildings.

The city itself seemed similar to our world—with some exceptions. One of the more obvious was that there were no cars. Everyone walked or occasionally "glided" to their destinations. Another major difference, especially from the big city I had lived in, was that everything was immaculate. No filth or trash was seen in the streets. Also, there were no curbs or gutters. Many of the streets and smaller walkways seemed to be made out of some kind of flat paving stone. Gorgeous flowers were everywhere lining the walkways. All areas were surrounded with fountains and streams. The scenery was enhanced with perfectly trimmed shrubbery and hedges, making it all very lovely and pleasing to look at. The more I looked down into the city, the more excited and anxious I became to go down into the city and be a part of the happiness and love I felt existed there, but I was not to be given that opportunity.

THE BUILDINGS

The buildings in the distance I now viewed from close up, and they were magnificent. The tallest of the buildings stood maybe three or four stories high, though most were only one level. They were of various architectural styles. One of the most common designs reminded me a little of Hearst Castle in California. I once watched a special televised tour of it with its marble floors, columns, pools, and fountains. Some of the buildings I now viewed had a slight resemblance to that structure. However, unlike the Hearst Castle with its elaborate furnishings, there were no statues, paintings, or artwork of any kind other than the beautifully carved furniture in the buildings. And yet, even the grandeur of Hearst Castle pales in comparison to the beauty of any of the structures I saw in the city. The buildings, flowers, shrubbery, and the shimmering fountains of water within the city were beyond anything that can be seen on this planet.

The buildings had the appearance of a pinkish-white alabaster or marble so thin that it looked almost transparent. As I concentrated on one of the buildings, I could see right through its walls. Inside, I saw columns and steps and many rooms with large hallways. These corridors were very wide and full of people going places. Fifty people could easily have stood shoulder to shoulder across the width. The rooms were even larger and filled with hundreds of people.

Even though I had come to disbelieve in a life after death and all that was involved with that belief, I had always assumed that if there were a heaven it would be beautiful, and everyone would wear white. That was surely an apt description of the beauty of the world I happened upon, and yet one of the concepts I learned while asking questions on the hill previously was that this place, in all its magnificence, was not heaven. This was only a waiting place for the spirits of people who have departed from the earth while waiting for a future time when they would be assigned another place or kingdom. I understood that these other kingdoms of glory were more splendid than this temporary one.

The spirit world was divided into different levels, and there also came understanding that the kingdoms of glory contained levels, each being more beautiful and glorious than the one before it, until reaching the highest level where God the Father and Jesus Christ actually dwell. When the time of the resurrection and judgment comes, every spirit will be assigned to a level within one of these kingdoms according to the choices they made.

God is our Father in Heaven and we are literally sons and daughters of this deity. I learned that He and Jesus Christ are two separate, glorified beings.

Having seen the beauty of the waiting place for spirits, I cannot imagine the grandeur of the mansions where our Father and Jesus live. I would gladly have stayed in the world I had just encountered forever. I could not dream of a kingdom more glorious than this one.

THE PEOPLE AND ACTIVITIES IN THE CITY

As I mentioned before, even while looking down into the city from a great distance I could feel the love that was exchanged between the people as they greeted each other and conversed. The parklike spaces between the buildings were vast, and I understood that the small groups of people gathered together were families and friends from earth. It came to me that most activities the people took part in were done within these groups, and I found comfort in knowing that I would continue friendships with those I had known while on earth.

There were so many people, and now I noticed the detail of their apparel. As a child when I thought about it, I assumed that people in Heaven would only wear white. At least that was the way Heaven was depicted in stories I had been told. However, I observed that while some apparently do choose white, many of the people wore beautiful pastel robes. Both men and women wore the same style of clothing, made of shimmering fabric similar to silk but much finer. The fabric glowed and appeared like spun light. The robes were long, down to the ankle, and slit a little up the side almost to the knee.

38

They wore cummerbunds around their waists and long shawls of various pastel colors over their shoulders. The shawls hung down to the ground.

I also saw a few men wearing dark suits. I am not sure why but learned that when spirit beings appear to loved-ones back on earth, they will often appear in the same apparel they were buried in or last seen in so that they can be recognized.

Another thing that I noticed was that the people gave off their own light. The glow varied from person to person, and a few were of a more distinctive golden hue. When I asked about the difference in illumination between the people, I learned that their light was in direct proportion to how each individual had lived their life while on earth. This answer seemed to satisfy my curiosity for the time being.

THE "KITCHEN"

In one of the very large rooms in the building I was looking at, or looking through, I saw a large group of women involved in some very specific tasks. They were quietly talking and laughing as they worked. Most of their communication was done telepathically or in whispers. My interest was seized by this group because of the pleasure they appeared to have found in what they were doing. They were having a wonderful time and I became curious as to what they were doing.

On closer inspection I realized that they were preparing food, and the room they were in was a very large kitchen. Some of the women were slicing what appeared to be a fruit, shaped somewhat like a pear that also glowed, and arranging the slices on platters that had the look of crystal glass. Others were slicing and arranging what looked like little wafers of a cakelike bread. The wafers, or minicakes, were of a spongy texture and the size and shape of a hard boiled egg and when sliced were about a quarter of an inch in thickness. I watched as one of the women occasionally tasted a wafer as she made the arrangement. I wished that I could taste one too, and instantly a wafer was literally melting in my mouth. The taste of it was exquisite. More than just a taste or flavor, eating the wafer made me feel good and happy all at the same time. The taste was extremely intense as was everything else. As I watched this activity, I was impressed that people ate more for pleasure than for sustenance.

THE LIBRARY

Looking along another corridor, I saw people going in and out of another very large room. The room appeared to be a library, since it had row after row of huge books along all of the walls. I would guess the books were about five or six inches thick and fourteen inches high. They appeared to be beautifully bound and engraved with something that I do not think was leather, though it was dark brown in color. People stood studying and reading at ornate, intricately carved tables while others walked about normally. It was here I noticed that there were no chairs anywhere. This seemed strange, since I had seen people sitting on the lawn while caught up in conversation outside earlier. As I thought about this I was impressed with the understanding that chairs were not needed here except for some kinds of work, since people never grew tired and had no need to sit and rest.

I should mention that as I was looking down this corridor and into the rooms, I heard music playing. I am reluctant to describe the instruments that made the music as harps; however, that is exactly what they sounded like. The music was heavenly and offered a soothing or comforting background to the many activities in which people took part.

A PERSON REPENTING

After this, I glanced quickly into another area, generally seeing the same kind of activities taking place. But then I saw something that caught my attention. The room was not very large, especially compared to the others I had seen, and there appeared to be only one person in the room. He was sitting in a chair that was like a console in front of a large screen the size of one of the walls. It was not like a big TV or even a computer. I can only try to describe it as being transparent, and it appeared to be made out of a gel or liquid that stayed stationery. It was large and oblong with rounded corners. As I concentrated I could see that there was a man in it, or rather the image of a man. As I focused on the man for a moment, I was given to understand that the person I saw was still alive and living on the earth and that this was a view of his spirit-self.

While I watched, the worker sitting at the console removed a long, colored, shaped object from one part of the module. It was about four or five inches long and about an inch in diameter. It was flat on one end, pointed on the other, and glowed slightly. He then placed the object into an opening on the console. He repeated this process a couple of times with other objects of different colors but all of the same shape. As I saw this going on I asked in my mind what was happening. What was this man at the console doing? The answer presented to me was that this man's life, whose image

41

There Is No Death

I saw was being revised. He was repenting, and what he had done wrong was literally being wiped off this screen. I was witnessing the method used to record what seemed like a kind of "spiritual DNA." I immediately understood that this is what is referred to in the scriptures as the "Book of Life." Everything that a person says, does, or thinks from the time they are born to the day they die is recorded in their own soul, not written down by some heavenly being as we may have thought.

I now grasped the concept that because of these recordings in our spiritual DNA, when we pass from this life we will be able to look at another being in the spirit world and "read" their life. The light or glowing I noticed coming from the people earlier was a part of this recording, and I understood that if I concentrated a little harder I could read the entire life history of each person I focused on.

I understood further that the more righteous or Godlike a person had been on earth—the more he or she had tried to obey God and help others—the brighter would be his or her light in the spirit world. The only parts of a person's life that would not be seen or read would be those sins that had been repented of the way the man on the screen was doing. A person having repented may still remember the deleted segments of their life, but those details would be kept from others. I also realized that there was no casual interest in "looking into" people's lives.

Another concept I understood was that it is far easier to repent or change our lives while in the mortal world than it is after passing into the spirit world. When we make the transition we call death, which is referred to there as the "new birth," we

42

take with us our attitudes, passions, desires, habits, qualities, and character. We really don't change at all. Everything that makes us who we are comes with us as part of our soul essence or spiritual DNA. Included in our soul is this recording of all of our words and actions and experiences from the very beginning since that is part of who we really are.

However, once we are in the spirit world, all of our emotions and attitudes become greatly intensified, thereby increasing the difficulty involved in changing them. I was also informed that if this man on the screen again committed these same sins of which he was repenting, the parts that had been removed would be replaced, and all that had been erased would once again be present in his recording for all to read.

As these thoughts and explanations came into my mind, I became frightened. There were parts of my life I definitely did not want others to see, and now, in dismay, I realized I could not hide anything from anyone.

MY LIFE'S REVIEW

At that moment I started thinking about all of the things that I had done in my life. As the thoughts formed in my mind, a window seemed to open before me and my life's review began. The window appeared to be several inches wide and opened like a scroll in front of me. It was as if someone had a video that ran at fast-forward, showing my entire life from my birth until the moment I arrived in the spirit world. It only took seconds, and yet I was doing more than just watching the events of my life pass by. With each event I not only saw my actions, but I heard the thoughts I was thinking and felt what I was feeling at the time. I was reliving each experience, only this time I could see all that was happening around me as well. I could see and feel what those I interacted with were seeing and feeling. I could actually feel their pain or joy and understand what they were thinking as they reacted to my actions. For me, this was not a pleasant experience.

There were some good things I had done in life but very few. I began to feel sick and full of pain because of the things I had done and the pains of the heart I had inflicted upon others. Despair set in because I felt sure I would never be able to undo any of my misdeeds. As I viewed my life, there was no doubt in me about what was good or bad. I could no longer lie to myself or anyone else about my feelings or motives. The worst parts of the review were when I had intentionally hurt someone else. Somehow the emotions of the moment combined, and I felt not only my anguish but also the pain felt by others. I was in misery.

Quickly I came to understand two very important concepts: The first was that I alone am responsible for my actions. When I had my life's review, I could not blame others for what I had done. Each of us decides his or her actions. Even if you had been abused, as I was, there would be no excuse for treating others the same way.

The second was that our thoughts, words, and actions are extremely powerful and have an effect upon more people than we realize. Like the far-reaching ripples in a pond after a rock is thrown in, the effects of our actions touch people that we are not even aware of. But unlike the ripples in a pond, the ripples or effects of our life's actions also come back to us, for good or bad. If we have had good thoughts and actions that helped and lifted others, we will feel the benefits as they ripple back to us. Unfortunately the opposite is also true. Acts of unkindness and cruelty will have their negative impact upon us as well.

As I watched the actions of my life in review, I became ashamed of many of the things I had done and began to feel the pain personally that I inflicted upon others during the course of my life. To help give understanding to some degree of what I was feeling, I will relate one small incident. Believe me when I say that there were many things worse than this one episode, but hopefully it will show the pain caused by one seemingly insignificant event and also help in understanding what I felt at that time.

During my life this one incident seemed insignificant. I had mistreated a girl I knew while living in one of my "foster" homes. I had long forgotten her and what I had done to her, but now in my review it was all there. I remembered every action and every cruelty.

At the time I was 14 years old and enjoying the greatest happiness I had ever known living with Joanne and her family. When I moved into their home I owned a few cotton dresses (which I had sewn myself which were in very poor condition) and a pair of tennis shoes. Joanne and her sisters had nice clothes that appeared absolutely perfect to me. Upon my arrival Joanne threw open her closet doors and said, "What is mine is now yours. Wear anything you want." This seemed incredible to me and so different from my past experiences, but I was grateful and began sharing this lovely wardrobe. My new "sister" was very popular at school and her church and was always surrounded by lots of friends. Since I was now part of her family, I was included in the popular groups.

During this time, another girl that the world would consider unattractive was attending both our school and church. She was overweight and had dark, bushy eyebrows as well as a rough complexion and some visible facial hair.

Everyone in our popular crowd made fun of Rachel. She was the object of many rude comments and jokes. Though Joanne and I never said anything to her face as many others did (and thank God I was never that cruel), we were unkind behind her back. We purposely excluded her from almost all of the activities that we were involved in, including social gatherings that took place in my new home. In short, we were not very nice to her, and my hypocrisy and lack of kindness came through very loud and clear during my life's review. Here I was a skinny, little, poor, white-trash girl that, through the mercy of one kind, religious family, had been taken in, dressed up, and accepted into the "in" group. We, my sister and I, had shut out another.

I never before realized how much I hurt Rachel by my actions, but during my life's review, I could feel the pain and heartache she felt as my insensitive actions affected her. I remembered one particular time when we snubbed her badly. Suddenly the pain of this one unkind act was so great for me to bear that I began to understand to a very small degree the agony of pain experienced by Jesus as he felt the sins of the world. My spirit-body felt as though it would disintegrate, so great was the pain I felt over this one memory. I hope that someday I can ask her forgiveness in person. I look at people very differently now than I did before I learned this valuable lesson. Our appearances here on earth are only temporary. Everyone's spirit is beautiful. I no longer see anyone as unattractive.

Since my return to mortality I have attempted to right as many of the wrongs as I possibly could. I have found people that I harmed in various ways—those I had gossiped or lied about—and humbly asked their forgiveness. A couple of years ago I visited a "foster" mother. She had been very mean to me while in her home. During this visit I was able to turn that experience around for good. Hopefully these steps will erase some of those events from my future life's review.

I still cannot forget what I felt as I watched my life's recording, but I realized that what I felt that day was only a small glimpse of what I would have felt had I passed through the "film" to remain permanently in the spirit world. I saw incidents and events in that review that I had completely forgotten, including those so small that they seemed insignificant, yet there they were—every detail, good or bad, pertaining to my probation while on earth.

There are still things in my life left undone, so to speak, which cause me great pain—mistakes I cannot make right with others—and so I have asked the Lord in prayer to please help me and forgive me for those things I cannot change. The greatest challenge I face is to forgive myself as I remember vividly the details of my life prior to my earthly departure.

CHRIST ENTERS THE CITY

Upon completing my life's review, which took only seconds, I felt sickened and was left extremely shaken. It was then that I noticed something going on in the distant city that caught my attention. An extremely bright light had entered the city and was gradually moving down one of the streets. This moving light was so brilliant that it outshone the light of the city and was blinding beyond our sun or any other light source I am familiar with. It was so much brighter than anything or anyone else around it. It was then that I realized the source of this moving light was a man at its center. He was walking with a crowd of people all around Him. The light came from Him, from His body and His clothing. It was like He and His clothing were made of brilliant light. Immediately around His person there was a golden glow with beams of sparkling light pouring from His body and reaching out a considerable distance. As I looked closer at this sparkling golden light, it appeared like fragmented gold dust was actually a part of the beams.

The man was incredibly beautiful, and then in an instant I knew that this was Jesus Christ making a visit to the city. He didn't appear at all like the pictures we often see of Him. He had no beard, and His hair was a reddish golden blond, and His eyes were a piercing blue. But, like most things in the spirit world, it wasn't His appearance that was so overpowering; it was the feelings of love and complete acceptance transmitted to me as I gazed upon Him. The feelings were glorious beyond description and filled my whole being so that it felt as if it would burst.

As Jesus walked down the streets, people gathered around Him in a huge crowd of hundreds, and yet there was no pushing as they reverently and courteously came as close to the Savior as they could. Those in positions closest to Him touched His clothes or his person and some embraced Him.

While observing the people, I knew that they were feeling His great love for them as I was feeling it. Those who could not get close enough to touch Jesus could feel His love through the golden beams of light emanating from Him. I thought to myself that these beams of light must spread throughout the universe and to us on earth as well, so that all people everywhere could feel this tremendous love if they wanted to. It was as if love was emanating from Him, permeating time and space, even in his physical absence.

As I looked down upon this scene, only one person in the city looked back at me. He was a handsome young man with dark hair and dark eyes, and he caught my attention just for a moment. I was impressed with the feeling that he was to be my child. I thought that could not come to fruition because I should not have any more children due to my diabetes, and I was now in a place where this would be impossible. This thought lasted for just a moment, and then he turned back toward the Savior. The full understanding of this experience came later in my life.

I AM GREETED BY A BEAUTIFUL WOMAN

At that moment I wanted nothing more than to go down into the city. I do not know if my intent was to ask the Savior's forgiveness through my tears or merely to embrace Him and bask in His love. I needed so desperately at that moment to feel His forgiveness and love in the despondent aftermath of my life's review. Before I was able to begin movement toward the city, however, out the back of my head I could see a beautiful woman coming up a path behind me.

I recognized powerfully at this time that I could see with every part of my body, not just with my eyes. I was aware of what was happening all around me. I could even see out of my fingertips. It was strange and wonderful to have that remarkable spirit body, a thing of light and substance beyond

49

earthly description and capable of doing so much more than our bodies of flesh.

As this angelic woman approached nearer, I turned around to face her. Her hair was a dark blond and swirled up on her head in the style of what we call a "French twist." She had on a peach-colored robe with a turquoise cummerbund around her waist and a cream-colored shawl draped over her shoulder and hanging down to the ground. She was wearing no shoes. Her robe had a soft, glimmering sheerness to it that seemed to be transparent yet was actually opaque.

I did not recognize her, though she seemed somewhat familiar. I felt I should know her but had no idea who she was. As I looked at her I was somehow able to determine that she was an older woman, even though she looked to be about thirty years old. Another wonderful thing I understood about spirit bodies was that they all looked to be about the same age. They were all absolutely beautiful and perfect, and while it was easy to tell them apart by their individual physical features, it was also possible to recognize each other spirit to spirit.

Upon reaching me, she said with surprise, "La Nelle, what are you doing here?" I questioned how she knew who I was. I understood in the intuitive way I had come to expect by now that there was something like a kind of signal that alerts family members in the spirit world when a relative on earth is about to die or "cross over." This provides the opportunity for them to be there and dress the new arrival, sometimes even before he or she leaves their body. This woman, whom I did not know, was a relative of mine. She had been caught by surprise, somehow knowing that it wasn't my time to cross over, so she had hurried to reach me. (See also page 129.)

I tried to grasp the thought that it wasn't my time to die, and more understanding began to flood into my mind. Apparently all of us have an allotted length of time to spend on the earth. No righteous person in this world dies before his or her time. So when a beautiful little child dies, or a beloved grandma or grandpa, or a sixteen-year-old nephew or sweet neighbor, we should not be overly grieved. If they were good people their death is correct according to their plan, even though it may be a time of sadness to those left behind. Sometimes a person's time can be cut short by use of drugs or other poor choices regarding how they care for their body. They lose the benefit of that time on earth. But, as I perceived it, the timing is more important than the way or manner a person dies.

I also understood that we have the choice or option to shorten our allotted time. I had tried to do so by committing suicide, but it was a very great sin and a terrible action to take. I thought about my death and immediately realized that for many suicides there is a great penalty or price that has to be paid. My understanding was that there are different kinds of suicides, and so they are judged differently. Some individuals are not in control of their minds when they make such a decision, and judgment for them would be very different as opposed to those who kill themselves so they will not get caught for some terrible crime they have committed.

Jesus knows and understands all of the circumstances present that cause a person to take such a drastic measure, even though committing suicide for any reason is very wrong. He takes all of that into consideration as no one else can when making assignments in the spirit world. Assignments may not really be the correct word because it seems to indicate decisions made on our

51

behalf by someone else. Quite the opposite is true as our assignments are determined by the choices we have made and how we have lived here on earth.

This entire chain of thoughts passed through my mind in the time it took this beautiful spirit woman to hesitate between words. She continued, "You cannot stay here. You have to go back." At this I started to cry because I had planned on going down to the city and wanted with all my heart to see the Savior and ease the pain I was feeling. I protested, "I don't want to go back. I don't want to go back."

Just then I felt something pulling at me like a huge vacuum cleaner sucking me into a void, and before I could say or do anything else, I found myself in another part of the spirit world—the place many refer to as hell.

CHAPTER 3

I VISIT "HELL"

"An Absolutely Terrible Place of Darkness and Despair"

The following descriptions of my death experience are without a doubt the most significant to me. Though I saw wondrous things, experienced the amazing abilities of the spirit body, and viewed future world events, the singular, life-changing event in all of this was the time I spent in a place we on earth commonly refer to as "hell."

TOTAL DARKNESS
AND OVERWHELMING SOUNDS

In a moment I once again changed locations. This time I was transported to a place of near-total darkness with shades of gray and black. Several things hit me all at once, and the total impact of it all was almost ferocious in its intensity. All of my newly discovered senses were bombarded with a heavy, overwhelming fear.

The first impression was that I had been in a world of extremely bright, penetrating light and now found myself surrounded by almost complete darkness. But it was more and much worse than mere darkness. It was an oppressive physical weight that I could feel pressing upon all of my body.

The cries around me were something I felt with my whole being rather than just heard. They were awful and reached into my core, filling me with a sense of fear and horror. At first I thought the sounds were those of tortured animals wailing in pain, but I quickly realized almost in shock that these unbelievable sounds were coming from people. Many were sobbing hysterically. Still others were wailing and grinding their teeth in terrible anguish that was caused not by physical pain, but by an inner, self-inflicted torment because of the weight of their sins.

About the same time that I recognized the source of the sounds that penetrated my entire being, I became aware of shapes moving in the blackness. I found that if I concentrated I could make out the silhouettes of these beings, the very ones who were making these pitiful, mournful, and almost inhuman sounds.

As I moved about, I could actually feel the "air" surrounding my body as it relentlessly clung around me like thick whipped cream. I started to feel claustrophobic, like a person drowning in thick, heavy goo. Into my mind it came that the "air" I was feeling was actually some kind of a tangible substance that locked these spirits into this place and did not allow them to cross over into the beautiful part of the spirit world where I had previously been. It was something like or related to the "film" I observed twice in the place of beauty, though it was different in its function.

Slowly moving about in this awful place, surrounded by the darkness and feeling with all of my senses the cries of these tormented spirits, I asked in my mind, Am I in Hell?

MY QUESTIONS ARE ANSWERED

The answer came quickly. No, this is not Hell, exactly. This was a place of temporary confinement for those spirits who had committed acts of evil during their lives on earth and, having not repented of them, had to suffer for their choices. Here they suffered a penalty for their sins that would help them understand the broad consequences of evil. People on earth referred to this place as hell because it is so very horrifying, but here they called it spirit prison. I understood that there were several areas to this spirit prison, and I was in the worst part of this place of sorrow. I was also impressed with the thought that the entire spirit prison was huge, perhaps even larger than the beautiful, peaceful spirit world.

People who had committed heinous, horrible crimes against other human beings were locked into this terrible place where they would for a period of time feel the pain they had inflicted upon others, but that pain was enormously multiplied. They were in an agony beyond mortal comprehension. I also understood that many of those held there were still filled with the hate and anger that had consumed them while upon the earth. I was somehow permitted to feel a small part of their emotions. The desires to murder, inflict pain, and destroy that they felt in their earth lives had remained with them, but they were now prevented from committing those acts because of their spirit nature. I understood that you could not physically hurt a spirit, good or evil.

I asked, How could a loving God put any of His children in a place like this no matter what they had done? The answer came immediately to me: God did not put them in this place. Their own actions drew them here. I then understood that somehow their evil deeds and desires while in mortality caused them to be attracted and pulled to this dreadful fate. I didn't exactly understand how that worked, but the answer satisfied me.

THERE IS NO LIGHT HERE

The reason it was so dark was because the people who were here, which included murderers, adulterers, rapists, and child molesters along with many others, had no light coming from their bodies. In the spirit world where I just came from, the plants, animals, buildings, and especially the people all had light coming from them. That is why they didn't need to have a sun or a star to give them light. They all produced their own by means of their goodness. I then remembered that in the spirit world I had not seen a sun in the sky, but everything was bright as if it had been in the middle of the day. Here in spirit prison it was so dark because the people were dark. They had rejected the light of God and turned against it and therefore it wasn't in them.

While feeling overwhelmed by my surroundings, something very strange seemed to come over me. I began to feel very badly for them. The strangeness of what I was feeling was the fact that I had never felt sympathy for anyone back on earth. My attitude had always been that it was a dog-eat-dog world, and I was going to take care of myself and let everyone else get along the best they could. But here I was feeling sincere empathy and concern for those around me. I wanted to help them in some way, but there was nothing I could do.

I wondered how long they would have to stay and instantly knew that some of them had already been there for a very long time—over a thousand years as time is measured on earth. Many others would stay perhaps for another thousand years or until they had fully repented of the things they had done. But at the same time I knew it was more than just repenting or changing their desires so they would not do those things any more. They were paying a price, the consequences of their own actions, in some sort of cosmic, spiritual way. What they had put out on earth was now coming back to them.

Remembering my own faults, I became extremely frightened. I asked, Am I going to have to stay here for the things I have done? I was terrified at the thought of staying in this awful place. I knew that I could not stand to be there for any amount of time, let alone a thousand years. I began to feel tremendous anxiety at the thought of having to remain with these people. I cried in my heart, I cannot stay here! Is this where I am going to be for a thousand years? Must I stay in this hell until I have paid the price for the actions and choices of my life?

I STAND NEXT TO MY FATHER

At that exact moment I felt my father standing next to me. I did not turn to look at him. However, I could feel his presence, and there was no doubt in my mind that it was my father. Suddenly, for some purpose, I was allowed to feel a small part of the pain that he was feeling for the life he lived. It was so completely overwhelming and excruciating that even twenty-two years after that experience I can still feel the pain my father felt.

I could not bear to look at him, but I began to feel great compassion for him. As I stood there listening to him crying and feeling his horrific pain, the spirit of hate that had been my constant companion during life, causing me to hate him and everyone else, suddenly and inexplicably left me. I truly felt God remove the sword of hate out of my hand.

I felt so sorry for my father that I wanted to put my arms around him, perhaps to give him some comfort of understanding that I had forgiven him, but I didn't. Because I couldn't touch him, I just stood there feeling his desire to change what he had done to me. Now he had real sorrow for his choices and the pain he inflicted on others. I realized that he was repenting, but it was excruciatingly painful and slow. It would take a very long time.

Once again I realized that we not only feel the pain of what we have personally done in our lives, but we also feel the pain that we have inflicted upon others—from their perspective. The unspeakable regret and torment these spirits were suffering was because of this ability to feel what others feel.

Many times we feel justified in taking revenge on those who hurt us by cheating us in business, personal relationships, or otherwise. We want assurance that they understand how much they have wronged us. The time will come when they will have a perfect knowledge of how we were affected by what they did. It is our responsibility to forgive them and let natural processes be the teacher. Also, we do not have the ability to accurately judge another's motives. We need to allow God to make those judgments.

Somehow I then knew that I was going to return to mortality. At that moment the thought of going back into my "clay body" and the miserable life I had led sounded pretty good—anything to get out of this horrible place. Even the trials of life were better than where I was.

CHAPTER 4

I SEE THE FUTURE

"I SEE MANY EVENTS THAT WILL SOON HAPPEN IN THE WORLD."

As I turned away from the black surroundings, a small light started to shine in front of me. The darkness, sounds, and feelings that had so completely oppressed me started to fade into the background. The light grew bigger, and a window opened up much the same as when I witnessed my life's review. This time, however, a panoramic view of the entire earth lay before me. It came closer and closer, as if I had been out in space and was flying toward it.

I knew that what was happening was intended to help me make my decision about going back to earth. A part of me wanted to go back to the beautiful spirit world, or paradise. Another part of me felt the need to be reunited with my body so I could change my life. It was a tug-of-war, and what I was about to see was to help me understand what I would be going through if I chose to go back into my "body of clay."

Again the view before me played out like a video in fast-forward motion, and yet I could see the scene in perfect clarity and was able to comprehend everything that transpired. As the earth zoomed up into my view, I first saw the whole world and then the various countries. It was made clear to me that in the future there would be wars and calamities, including nuclear attacks in various places in the world. A view of how it would start was given.

ISRAEL IS ATTACKED, A WORLD WAR BEGINS

I am not familiar with the geography of the world, but as I looked at the various lands, I instinctively knew what countries they were. Looking at the Middle East, I watched as a missile flew from Libya and hit Israel. The mushroom cloud that resulted from the blast was visible, and I knew that the missile contained a nuclear bomb. I was aware that those responsible for the missile were Iranian, but the missile had been hidden and fired from within the borders of Libya.

Almost immediately other missiles began flying from one country to another, quickly spreading war around the world. I also saw that many nuclear explosions did not come from missiles but from bombs of some kind on the ground.

My focus then changed from the Middle East to the United States, and I understood that I was about to see some of the things that would lead up to the nuclear holocaust that I had just witnessed.

TALL BUILDINGS IN NEW YORK FALL

As I looked upon the continent of North America, I zeroed in on the East Coast and then on New York specifically. I saw New York City with all of its people and buildings. Then I saw some tall buildings crashing to the earth surrounded by tremendous billows of smoke, dust, and debris.

I zoomed in closer into the smoke and particles falling and saw a woman holding a little girl's hand and running from the crashing buildings. The woman had long, dark hair hanging past her shoulders and curled inward slightly. She wore a beige business suit, heels of a slightly darker color, perhaps tan, and she was not wearing glasses. The little girl appeared to be six or seven years old with short brown hair reaching below the chin and cut in a type of pageboy look. They ran together, holding hands and trying to escape from the falling buildings. As they ran through the heavy smoke and dust, they were forced to let go of their hands and became separated. The child was terrified, and I could hear her screaming, "Mommy, mommy!" over and over again.

I don't know their outcome, if they lived or died, but I can still see the face of the woman clearly and could easily identify her from a photo or describe her to a sketch artist. I wondered if an earthquake had caused the buildings to fall and felt impressed that the answer was No. However, I was not given any indication as to the cause of the destruction. As I watched the attack on the World Trade Center towers on September 11, 2001, it was like watching a rerun.

COMMERCE CEASES

The next thing that came to me was more felt than
seen. It was the understanding that shortly after the crashing of
the buildings in New York City, commerce ceased. Shopping
and buying seemed to stop, and the economy failed throughout
the world. Few had any money at all, and those who did have
it could not buy anything. Gold and silver and other
commodities had value and could be traded. However, as time
passed, precious metals and other items of value such as jewels
became worthless.

FOUR CITIES ATTACKED WITH DISEASE

I then saw a man walk into the middle of a crowd of
people and drop what seemed like a quart jar full of liquid. The
jar broke and the liquid spread. I understood that people
nearby had become infected with a disease from the liquid, and
they didn't even know it. A day or two later people became sick
and started dying. I saw that this would happen in four
particular cities: New York, Los Angeles, San Francisco, and Salt
Lake City. The disease started with white blisters, some of the
size of a dime, appearing on the hands, arms, and faces of the
victims. The blisters quickly developed into white sores,
apparently filled with pus. Those with the disease would
stumble around for weeks and fall over dead.

I also saw other people with a flulike virus that spread
more quickly than the first disease. The victims had blood
coming from their nose, mouth, eyes, and ears. These people
died even faster of this disease than the ones who had the first
sickness. These diseases became widespread across the United

States with hundreds of thousands infected. Many died within a short time, perhaps 24 hours.

MARAUDING GANGS AND CHAOS

As the people were fleeing the cities in the hope of saving their lives, gangs were attacking and killing them. In the towns that were struck with disease there was chaos with looting, rioting, and murders involved—a complete breakdown of society. Many people seemed to go crazy. I sensed that the electricity had failed everywhere and that nothing was operating throughout the country, including any of the communications systems. I watched people throw rocks through windows to steal TVs that would not work and thought it very strange.

While I watched this all happening in the United States, my view instantly jumped back to the Middle East, and I saw the same plagues transpiring in Israel. The same sores and the types of sickness and disease that were occurring in the United States had also been unleashed there.

THE LONG WINTER AND FAMINE

The switch in view only lasted an instant, and I was back to the United States. A tremendously long winter had caught everyone by surprise following the siege of sickness. It started early and lasted into the summer months. A famine had begun over the few years leading up to the long winter because of storms, droughts, floods, and other plagues that had taken place. And the abnormally long cold period seemed to cause the famine to suddenly increase to its full measure.

Not long after this period of time following the diseases and long winter, events began quickly occurring in sequence, one right after the other. My sense of timing was not very clear at this moment because I was seeing several things happen all at the same time or very close together.

During and after the long winter, the disease spread in every state and increased in severity. The economy and the electricity were completely gone. Chaos and anarchy reigned over the entire country because, without any governmental structure, there was a total breakdown. I saw people's hearts fail them from fear. Almost everyone was searching in a desperate attempt to find some food. There was an extreme shortage everywhere but in some areas there was no food at all. In these places I could see people so hungry they were digging in the ground for worms.

DEADLY WATER

Also during this time, I became aware that there was very little drinking water and that the remaining water had become contaminated. If a person drank it they would contact the disease and die. Because of their great thirst, many people drank the water in spite of the danger of poisoning.

I mentioned earlier about the gangs that killed people trying to escape the cities. It seemed that some of them had lost their minds and went around in these gangs killing people just for the sake of killing; others did so for food or to gain some material possessions from their victims. Those who were killing for no reason were like beasts—animals completely out of control as they raped, looted, burned, and butchered people. I saw these gangs go into the homes of those who were hiding. They would drag them out of their hiding places and commit unspeakable horrors.

An unnatural fear and hatred came over many people. Some family ties that once existed between husbands and wives and parents and children no longer mattered. They only cared about individual survival. Men would kill their wives and children for food or water. Mothers would kill their children. The events that then lay before me were horrible beyond description and almost unbearable to watch.

CITIES OF LIGHT AND SAFETY

The air everywhere seemed to be filled with smoke as many buildings and cities burned with no one attempting to control the fires. As I looked upon this scene of chaos, smoke, and destruction, I noticed that there were small pockets of light scattered over the United States, perhaps 20 or 30 of them. I noticed that most of the locations of light were in the western part of the United States with only three or four of them being in the East. These places of light seemed to shine brightly through the darkness and were such a contrast to the rest of the scene that they caught my full attention. I focused on them for a moment and asked, *What is this light?*

I was then able to see that these points of light were people who had gathered together and were kneeling in prayer. The light was actually coming from the people, and I understood that it was showing forth their goodness and love for each other. They had gathered together for safety and, contrary to what I had witnessed elsewhere, were caring more

67

for each other than for themselves. Some of the groups were small with only a hundred people or so. Other groups consisted of what seemed to be thousands.

I realized that many, if not all, of these places of light, or cities of light (as I began to think of them) had somehow been established just before most of the devastations and that they were very organized. It was as if they had known what was coming and had prepared for it. I did not see who or what had organized them, but I did see many people struggling to reach them with nothing but what they could carry.

In contrast to the outside areas, these cities of light had food that was readily shared with those who joined them. In these places there was relative peace and safety. The inhabitants were living in tents of all kinds, many of which were no more than blankets held up by poles. I noticed that the gangs made no threats on these groups and left them completely alone, choosing to pick on easier targets and unprotected people. Many were attacked who were trying to reach these cities. However, the people within had defenses and God was with them.

I realized that these cities of light were temporary, and that in a short time the people living within them would go to another place. I do not know where they were to go but seemed to think that they were to gather in the mountains—to higher places.

THE NUCLEAR ATTACK ON THE UNITED STATES

While viewing the cities of light, my focus changed and I became aware of missiles being launched and hitting United

States cities. I watched as mushroom clouds started forming over many areas of the States. Some of the clouds came from missiles that I knew were fired from Russia, and others were not from missiles at all but from bombs that were already within the country. These latter bombs had been hidden in trucks and cars and were driven to certain locations and then detonated.

I specifically saw Los Angeles, Las Vegas, and New York City hit with bombs. New York City was hit with a missile, but I think Los Angeles was hit by at least one truck bomb, if not several, because I did not see any missile. I also saw a small mushroom cloud form north of Salt Lake City without the aid of a missile.

In the darkness I also saw fireballs falling from the sky. This took place after the mushroom clouds. The balls fell from the sky, were of different sizes—most being the size of golf balls—and were very hot. There were millions of them. As they fell from the sky, they left streaks of flame and smoke behind them. Everything they touched started on fire: people, buildings, trees, and grass. Everything burned. I didn't ask what they were or where they had come from because by this time I was sick over the scene before me. From here on I observed without asking many questions.

NORTH AMERICA INVADED

At almost the same time and in the same locations as the mushroom clouds, I saw Russian and Chinese troops invading the United States. The Russians were parachuting into many spots along the Eastern Coast. I also saw them parachuting into Utah. Chinese troops were invading from the

West Coast near Los Angeles. They were met with resistance from those who had survived the disease and bombs. I did not see any United States military there at that time.

This invasion was part of the nuclear war that I had seen earlier, and I knew that similar events were taking place all over the world as I had seen previously. I did not see much of this war but was impressed that it was short in duration and that the Russian and Chinese armies were defeated and withdrew. No explanation regarding how or why was received.

THE EARTH CLEANSES ITSELF

Now the smoke became very heavy, dark, and thick. Just as things appeared to be as bad as they could get, the earth began to quake. This occurred during a winter, seemingly the winter that followed the very long one I had seen earlier. The chaos had existed for almost a full year by this time. The earthquakes began in the West, around Idaho and Wyoming, and then quickly spread in every direction. I saw a huge earthquake hit Utah and then California. Earthquakes happened all over California, but they were especially devastating in the Los Angeles and San Francisco areas. San Francisco appeared to turn upside down. The multiple earthquakes triggered volcanoes all over the West, and they started spewing a tremendous amount of ash and smoke into the air, causing it to become very dark and dirty and to block much of what was left of the sunlight. Huge waves of water swept over the West Coast. As I saw them, I realized that this same destruction was happening to coastal cities all over the world. The waves were so huge that Los Angeles was nearly swept away.

I saw a wall of water taller than some of the buildings, perhaps as high as fifteen or twenty feet, sweep through Salt Lake City. I thought this strange because of its location so far from an ocean. I wondered how a wave could travel all the way to Salt Lake City. I was impressed that the wave had not originated at the ocean, but was from underground. I quickly noticed great cracks in the earth around Salt Lake City open up and saw water shooting up out of the ground. I felt that deep under the ground there was a huge amount of water and that the earthquakes had forced it up to the surface. Most of the buildings were swept away or destroyed when the water swept over the city. In fact, there was tremendous destruction, with only a few buildings left standing. The water coming from underground stretched from Idaho down to near Cedar City, Utah, and was very destructive.

As I looked, I could see that cities all over the country had been devastated, and rubble was everywhere. Most of the buildings were destroyed. However, I realized that even though there was tremendous destruction from earthquakes, disease, floods, volcanoes, and tidal waves, the majority of deaths were caused by the gangs of roving marauders that killed merely for pleasure.

As I studied this scene for a moment, the thought occurred to me that the earth itself had become sickened at the terrible acts of cruelty that were happening upon it and was finally reacting through these natural disasters. The earth was attempting to cleanse itself of the chaos and evil that engulfed the people. The ash and smoke from the volcanoes had increased, and now almost complete darkness was everywhere upon the earth.

The diseases also increased in devastation, and I saw people literally dying on their feet. I saw another particular disease that started with red blotches. The victims would quickly start to bleed from every opening in their bodies and then literally disintegrate or melt into unrecognizable masses of flesh and bone. The sight was horrendous because carnage and death were everywhere.

After this second terrible scene, I saw the survivors gather up the dead into huge piles to burn them. The stench was sickening. Some of the bodies had been burned during the time of chaos, but because people were more concerned with their survival, they had mostly ignored the dead around them.

FOUR MORE EVENTS

I then saw four additional events occur. One of these was a huge earthquake which occurred in the middle of the United States. It was tremendous and seemed to split the United States in half about where the Mississippi River is. The crack in the earth that resulted was huge, miles wide, and as it opened up the earth seemed to swallow everything. Water flowed in from the Gulf of Mexico all the way up to the Great Lakes. The Great Lakes did not exist any longer, however, because they became part of a large inland sea.

Another event was a series of tremendous earthquakes all over the world. One in particular was a large, worldwide quake that caused huge walls of water to sweep over all of the coastal regions. This earthquake and the walls of water made the earlier ones seem small by comparison. I am not sure if the earthquake that split the United States in two was a part of this worldwide quake or not.

I also saw a mighty wind come upon the earth. As the wind hit, I saw people go into caves and into the cracks of rocks and underground to try to escape its fury. It appeared to be stronger than any hurricane or tornado. It seemed that everything that had been left was now blown away. I understood, without asking, that the great worldwide earthquake and the mighty wind were somehow caused by a huge planetlike object that had come very close to the earth and had disrupted everything. It was also made clear to me that it was very near the "end" when this happened.

Now my perspective changed. I once again viewed the entire earth from a distance. I saw a huge fireball, much bigger than the earth, approaching our planet. It was extremely bright red and gold in color and engulfed the whole earth. When I witnessed this event, I could not help but feel the difference between it and everything else that occurred. I was impressed that it was the burning of the earth that is described in the Bible. I understood that just before the fireball's appearance, Jesus had appeared, and the good people I had seen earlier had gone with him and were no longer upon the earth. The few people left behind were those wicked individuals who had survived the earlier plagues and judgements.

The picture of the earth engulfed by this huge ball of red and gold fire slowly faded away into blackness. I realized at that moment that I had to go down and take care of my children so that they could be prepared for these terrible events that were going to happen. Everything that was shown to me came to a close and then I woke up in the hospital.

CHAPTER 5

MY RETURN TO MORTALITY

THE HOSPITAL

Like awakening from a bad dream, I gradually realized I was re-entering my physical body. Through this process I learned that even though the spirit is not in it, the body can still appear to be alive and functioning. There is a space or period of time that the spirit can be separated from the body, but the spirit must return within that time or it cannot enter again.

I could hear the sounds of a hospital emergency room and feel someone forcing an awful tasting liquid down my throat. I started throwing up and continued to do so again and again. Thus began my return to mortality. During the transition, I could still hear the cries of the spirits in Hell, but those quickly faded away.

While in the hospital, I was in turmoil. Part of me felt groggy and tired and wanted just to be left alone so that I could sleep. The other part of me didn't want to sleep for fear of forgetting what had happened. I was emotionally exhausted. Sleep won out most of the time, but thankfully I soon realized that I wasn't going to forget what I experienced and stopped worrying about it. Even though I spent the little waking time I had constantly thinking about what had happened, I didn't tell anyone at the hospital about it.

My medical stay lasted a couple of days, but no one came to visit me. At that time all my siblings lived in other states. I was tired and lonely and wanted to go home badly. I kept thinking how wonderful it would be to see my children and worried that there was no one at the apartment to feed my cat, which I dearly loved.

TWO WEEKS IN AN EARTHLY "PURGATORY"

In a couple of days, two very nice policemen arrived without warning and took me in their police vehicle away from the hospital. I thought they were taking me home. Instead they took me to a psychiatric facility in Hawthorne for the evaluation required by state law in cases involving suicide.

Immediately after I was admitted and as I stood there wondering what was going to happen to me, some men in white coats literally dragged a young girl in, screaming at the top of her lungs. They locked her in a room and went away. That event set the tone of my entire stay there. I was "incarcerated" together with a lot of drug addicts, drunks, runaways, and a few mentally disturbed people, both men and women. It was not a pleasant place to be.

I spent two weeks there and hated every minute of it. There was no privacy at all. We were always being watched, even when we took a shower. They kept repeating the same questions over and over again. It seemed as if they were just playing games with me. What a waste of my time! I just wanted to get out of there and go home and start my life over.

I soon learned that if I wanted to be released from that place I should tell them only what they wanted to hear, so I kept the information regarding my incredible and wonderful experience to myself. In fact, I lied to them so that I could get out of there faster. I said I hadn't committed suicide, but rather had been very stressed and took some medication to sleep. I don't think I fooled them. However, I did tell the lady psychiatrist questioning me that if I hadn't wanted to commit suicide before arriving at her facility, I definitely would have after being there a while.

The only thing that helped me keep my sanity during this time was that I remembered everything about my experience and thought about it constantly. It consumed me. I never questioned if it had been a dream or something I imagined. I knew without a doubt that it really happened. My problem was deciding what to do about it. I remembered my life's review and how badly I felt. I wanted desperately to "repent" like the man I had seen in the spirit world so that my sins would be blocked and couldn't be read, but I didn't know how to begin.

No friend or family member visited or called me during the time I was undergoing psychiatric evaluation. After two weeks I was discharged, and my oldest sister Sandra came and picked me up in her car. While we drove she didn't say a word; the silence was deafening. I felt I needed to say something to help her feel the same change and understanding that I now felt, especially towards my father. I wanted to help relieve the pain I knew she was feeling. After building up my courage I said, "It is important that you forgive my father for what he did to you. I know what happened to you." It must have been too difficult for her to talk about because she stared ahead and didn't respond. The atmosphere suddenly became very solemn. I didn't see or talk to my sister after that day until approximately ten years later.

I went back for a while to the apartment where I had been living. At first Shaun really didn't care about what happened to me. He was struggling so hard with his own problems that he didn't have time for anything or anyone else. His addiction was destroying him, and I wasn't sure I could help him. I was still depressed, confused, and tired—confused not concerning my experience, but about what I was going to do in life. I still didn't have a job, any money, or a place to live. At the same time I knew I had to make some serious changes within myself, but I still didn't have a clue about how or where to begin. Later Shaun did a lot to help me and my children get back together again. We are still friends today.

JOANNE TO THE RESCUE

About that time my "sister" Joanne came to my rescue once again, as she had many times before, allowing me to stay with her until I could get back on my feet. Joanne helped a lot and I slowly started coming out of my depression. I told her a little about my experience from time to time, a little bit here and a little bit there, but never the whole story until much later. Sharing the experience was not my focus—trying to deal with life was. After a few months I started functioning again and going to different churches and reading the New Testament daily. This helped me a lot. The Bible was now easier to understand and made sense to me. However, as I tried harder to change my life, new challenges arose.

I quickly realized that even though I had experienced something truly extraordinary, learned a tremendous number of important and precious truths, and was trying to change myself, my life was not going to be a bed of roses.

With Shaun's and Joanne's help, I continued rebuilding my life. Then one day I received notice that my ex-husband was suing me for sole custody of my youngest son, Glenn. In the suit I was characterized as an irresponsible, uneducated derelict, unfit to have or raise children. He used all my mistakes of the past against me. During the court proceedings I found that trials can be tremendously stressful and that truth does not always prevail. People who should have been committed to truth lied and misrepresented the facts.

I kept in contact with Shaun, who was still struggling to overcome his cocaine addiction. He was making some progress, and when I told him about my legal problems, he offered to hire an attorney for me. He was very sweet and paid thousands of dollars for a lawyer. After the dust settled, I had gone through one of the most difficult times of my life, but I miraculously won custody of my son. Shaun and I still communicate often. He has overcome his addiction and is doing quite well.

During this time I worked really hard on making changes. I had a lot of bad habits and attitudes that had to be overcome. The first thing to learn was to keep my mouth shut and not say anything negative. For a long time I didn't say a whole lot. Then I worked on changing my thoughts—even to the point of not thinking bad things about people. I tried hard not to judge anymore. Wanting to get a fresh start and move away from everything about my past, I moved my family out of California to a place I thought would be very safe and secure. I found a cute little home where I baked bread and grew a large and productive vegetable garden in the back yard. Our circumstances were improving.

MY SON IS KIDNAPPED

We had been in our new home about three or four months when one of the neighbors came running into the house we were renting. She was hysterical and blurted out that an old car with a man and a woman in it had pulled up along the sidewalk. The man got out and knocked the neighbor's child off of his bicycle while trying to grab my son. He jumped back into the car with my boy screaming and kicking and drove off. The only witness was the little boy who was too terrified to remember any important details.

I ran outside and fell to my knees and didn't even feel the sharpness of the gravel in the driveway. I felt as if my life had been ripped away from me. The police came but were not able to do much. After a very long and emotional two weeks, I received a telegram from my ex-husband. He said that he had taken his son and was going to raise him and that I would never see him again. I turned the telegram over to the police and went into a deep depression. My life had again taken an extreme turn for the worse, but this time it was different. During this dark period my experience sustained me and I had a glimmer of hope.

But even with this new outlook it was hard to be the mother I wanted to be to Sean and Chad.

(Ten years after he was kidnapped by his father, my son ran away and for a period of months searched until he found me. He now lives nearby, and he and his brothers visit me often.)

After another failed relationship I returned to Los Angeles where I started working at Twains, a cozy little coffee shop. A few years had passed since my suicide and life continued to gradually improve. I kept thinking about the things I experienced, and every once in a while I shared it with someone. I continued to improve myself and change my negative habits. I kept reading the Bible and took a renewed interest in studying various religions and in going to church. Some of my happiest memories are of things that happened at Twains during this period. I became good friends with so many wonderful people: Rick, Richie, Katie, and many other customers who were "regulars" and visited daily.

THE ASSAULT AND STABBING

While I was working in the coffee shop, a man came in every day and made it obvious that he was interested in me. He was persistent in asking me to go on a date with him, but I always replied with a polite "No, thank you; I'm not dating at this time." After a month or so, in one of our conversations I discovered that we had lived in the same area and had a few other interests in common. We went to dinner, and he frequently called on the phone.

81

I still barely knew him when he called and asked if I could come to his apartment and do some sewing for him. I expressed that I had been sick with the flu and was still recovering, but he insisted. As soon as I arrived, I sat down and took out my sewing supplies. He immediately walked over to me, slapped me hard on the face, and ripped open my blouse. He was aware that prior to meeting him I had been involved with a well-known actor named David, whom I still had feelings for. He was insanely jealous and told me to stop seeing him. He asked me several questions and no matter how I replied he would hit me in the head. I ran to the bathroom and locked the door, but he kicked it in. He then pulled a gun from the closet and put it to my head. I was pleading for my life for my children's sake, but he did not soften. He ordered me to remove my clothes and took out a knife. It was terrifying. Nothing I said would convince him to stop. At the point of succumbing to possible death, for some reason I said, "In the name of Jesus Christ, leave me alone." He stumbled back, and I was able to escape. My wounds were not life threatening, and I recovered physically very quickly. This man who sexually assaulted me went to prison for several years, mostly because he had been involved in a large burglary ring in the San Fernando Valley.

Again life dealt me a terrible blow, but I had changed a lot and reacted to it very differently. This traumatic assault could have crippled me emotionally, but the marvelous truths I learned on my spiritual journey, now becoming part of my life, helped me to quickly overcome the experience and move on.

I TELL MY EXPERIENCE TO FRANK

It was while working at Twains that I first told my full story to someone. Late one afternoon, an elderly man, who appeared to be in his seventies and down on his luck, came in and sat at my counter. As I went to take his order, I noticed that his hands were shaking really badly—so badly that he was spilling the coffee I had previously poured for him all over the counter. I asked him, "Are you all right?" He started crying right there in front of everyone. I waited a minute while he gained control of himself. He said, "A pretty girl like you wouldn't understand." I replied, "Yes, I would. I can understand your feelings. Please talk to me."

Slowly his dilemma came out. He didn't want to live anymore. He had been a top chef in some of the best restaurants in Los Angeles but had problems keeping a job because of his drinking. Then he had a terrible car accident one night when he was drunk and his wife of forty-plus years died in the crash. He could not forgive himself. Everything had fallen apart after that, and he had come to the end of his rope. He felt he had failed in everything he tried, and there was no reason left for him to live. Even though he had quit drinking, his circumstances had not improved. He felt he was a worthless bum, and he might as well end it all. He didn't know how to do it, but he was going to do it that night.

I told him, "Listen, I really need to tell you something very, very important, but I can't do it here. Will you promise me that you will not do anything tonight and come and let me make you dinner at my apartment tomorrow night? I want to tell you about something that will help you. Then after you listen to what I have to say, if you still want to commit suicide, I won't try to stop you."

He hesitated for a minute and then looked me in the eyes to see if I was "for real." I gave him my phone number and address and made him promise again not to do anything until after the next night. He told me his name was Frank.

The next night we had dinner, and I told him of my experience. I started with my life story and my suicide, and then I shared my entire visit to the spirit world. I told him everything. It truly touched him, and he went home saying he wasn't going to do anything other than just think about what I had told him. I also gave him a beautiful book of scripture, and he said he would read it.

He came into the restaurant every day after that. We became good friends and talked often, even after I moved out of California. It took him a while, but he started trying to put his life back together. He even started to take some classes at a community college in order to improve himself and got a job at a little fast food restaurant.

Seven years later I received a phone call from the Los Angeles Police Department saying that Frank had died of a heart attack. They found my name and phone number in his wallet and called me. They sent me some of his personal effects, including the book I had given him. He truly is in a much better place now, and I know that someday I will see my friend again.

ADVENTURES AT SYBIL BRAND

Shortly after I met Frank, my son Sean was back living with me, and we decided to move out of the state again. We left our apartment and moved most of our possessions into a storage unit in preparation for the move. I had worked and saved about a thousand dollars for the trip. As Sean and I were leaving town with personal items and the cat in the car, we were stopped by a police officer because he could not see the temporary registration in the back window. It had come loose and was folded over and not visible to him.

When he checked my license he found that there was a bench warrant out for my arrest. A few years earlier I had received a twenty-dollar traffic citation for not quite stopping at a stop sign, and with the confusion and hardships of life, and the ever-present shortness of funds, I had neglected to pay the ticket. I tried to explain the situation we were in, but it made no difference. I was handcuffed and hauled off to the nearest jail. The officer had no compunction for hauling me away and abandoning a fifteen-year-old boy who didn't have a place to stay, any money, or even a driver's license, to the streets of West LA.

This happened at about 11 a.m., and I wasn't actually booked into a facility until 2 a.m. the next morning. I was transferred three times before finally reaching Sybil Brand, which contained the worst of the worst criminals, murderers, prostitutes, drug dealers, and so forth. After a humiliating strip search and other indignities, I was taken to a cell. By this time I had not eaten and was starting to feel very weak from my diabetes. I desperately needed to give myself an insulin shot, but they had taken my insulin away from me—along with everything else. The next morning I was very sick. I was finally given some breakfast, and the jail nurse came to see me. She was a crusty, crude woman who had no visible signs of compassion whatsoever and refused to give me insulin.

85

She ignorantly asked, "How do you know you are diabetic?" I told her that I had been taking insulin for ten years and gave her my doctor's name. She did nothing, and within a short period of time I collapsed unconscious in a diabetic coma. My cellmates banged on the door to get the attention of the guards.

When the guards found me unconscious in my cell, they got the nurse to return. When she found me, she gave me a large injection of glucagon, a highly concentrated sugar solution, which was the absolute opposite of what I needed. Any trained nurse would have known that this was a serious mistake. Later I wondered if she had done it intentionally to cover her original medical blunder, as dead men tell no tales. I should have died, but I didn't. I was taken to the jail hospital and remained there in a coma for what I remember being about nine days.

After I regained consciousness, I was put back into the mainstream of the jail. Then I was placed in a "holding cell" to wait for a chance to see a judge. While there, I became weak and shaky and tried to tell the guards that I needed sugar or juice or something. I became more desperate and again banged on the door and begged them for help, but they only responded with lewd overtures and crude remarks. I have never heard worse taunting and harassing in my life. They called me a "junkie" and refused my request. It didn't help that I had bruises from the IVs still visible on my arm from my hospital stay while in the coma.

I went into insulin shock and convulsions and was eventually taken by ambulance back to the jail hospital. It took four or five days to stabilize after this ordeal. I was confined in a room with two prostitutes, one of whom continued to promise me that I would never make it out alive. A couple of days later I went before a judge and was at last released at 1 a.m. the next morning. While I was in court the prosecuting attorney told me that I had the makings of a multimillion dollar lawsuit. "But I didn't tell you that," he said.

I felt that those who were in charge of the prisoners at Sybil Brand were just as horrible as many of the people who were incarcerated there.

The crowning injustice was that the thousand dollars I had saved for moving out of California was now missing from my purse. I did not dare say anything about it at that point for fear of retribution. As soon as I was free I started calling friends to get a ride to someplace away from the jail and finally found a friend named Dan at home. Dan was willing and able to come and get me. The next morning, after some much-needed rest, I started calling friends to find Sean. He had been staying with a family we had befriended earlier.

After I found him and we were reunited, we spent the next three months living in my Volkswagen Beetle. Sean slept in the back seat, and I slept in the front. The cat was on the passenger-side floor. Sean went to school, and I worked at Twain's and gradually saved money so that we could eventually fulfill our dream and move out of state and into a house. At the time it was hard to see, but there was a silver lining behind all this, as can be seen by what happened next.

I ADOPT A SPECIAL BABY

Several months later, about two years after the assault, I met a young girl who was pregnant. I trained her as a waitress at

Twains and befriended her. She wanted to have an abortion, but I talked her out of it by agreeing to pay all the expenses of the birth and adopting the baby. For some reason I really wanted the baby. It took every dime I could scrape together for the adoption, including selling most of my furniture, but I felt it was worth it.

While the adoption was in process, a man whom I had never seen before came into the restaurant. He was friendly, and we started talking. It came out that I was working hard to earn enough money to pay for legal fees for the adoption. He said he would like to help. I politely turned him down a couple of times because I didn't know him and was afraid of doing something with "strings attached." The conversation turned to other things, and he left. The next day he showed up again and handed me an envelope. He said, "Just a little contribution to help." In it was two thousand dollars with a note saying it was for the baby. I never saw him again. I thanked the Lord with all my might for this miracle. It was after his birth that I realized this precious little baby was the spirit who had looked up at me from the city I visited in Paradise. I knew that God wanted me to name him Elias.

I LOSE MY SIGHT

Because of the goodness of several people, the adoption was finalized after three years. By now the two oldest boys had left home, leaving only my adopted child and me. I did not want to raise him in Los Angeles, so we moved out of state again. I found a job as a nanny in a large estate with a wonderful family. The husband was a plastic surgeon, and I was paid double what most other people in my field in this area were paid. His wife Lyn became my best friend.

During the next couple of years things went very well. We had sufficient for our needs, good friends, and finally peace. Elias and I were very happy. Then one day I woke up with a terrible headache and couldn't see; everything was a blur and I couldn't focus at all. It seemed like a layer of Vaseline was covering my eyes. I felt terrible and asked a friend to take me to the hospital. After an examination I was told that I was going blind as a result of my diabetes, and there was nothing I could do about it. I was told I could be completely blind within three or four months.

Elias at age 13

THE SWIRLING TUNNEL OF STARS

At this time I was better able to accept my current circumstance. I began developing skills needed by a person with limited sight. About a week later I woke up with a severe pain in my kidneys. It was so painful that I couldn't even reach the phone and dial. My five-year-old son Elias called my close friend Lyn who came right over to take me to the hospital. When she got there my face had gone to an ashen gray, and I became limp like a dishrag so that I had to be carried out to the car.

As we were speeding to the hospital in the car, Lyn was saying, "Hold on, Sarah, you're going to make it." I replied,

"No, I'm not. I am going to die this time. I see a swirling tunnel full of stars." I thought: I am going to really cross over this time, because now I see the tunnel that everyone always talks about. I wasn't afraid, but I was concerned for my little boy and wondered who would love and take care of him.

The hospital wasn't very far away, and they rushed me into the emergency room. When I regained consciousness a few minutes later, I was still in a lot of pain, but at least I was alive. I was told that my kidneys had failed. They were only working at about one percent. As I recuperated, I was informed that I would soon have to have a kidney transplant or start dialysis; otherwise, I would probably die within a couple of years.

I told them I had the faith to be healed if it was the Lord's will and that he would sustain me if I were meant to live. Otherwise, I was not afraid to go and so I did not want dialysis or a transplant at that time.

MY LIFE IS SPARED FOR A PURPOSE

While I was in the hospital recuperating, a close friend of mine, a minister, came and prayed and talked with me often. One day, after praying together, he told me that he felt very strongly that the Lord was sparing my life so that people would hear my voice. What he said surprised me. He didn't know about my near death experience and had no way of knowing what his words meant to me. I knew immediately in my heart that I needed to begin sharing what I had been blessed to learn so many years before. The year was 1992. (This wonderful, spiritual man passed away January 29, 2003.)

When the minister left, I thought a lot about what he said. I knew he was right, but I didn't know exactly where to start. After a day or two, I asked my doctor for permission to visit other patients on my floor, including several who were terminally ill. Earlier when I had been in the hospital, I had shared my experience with my physician. She thought for a moment and gave me the go-ahead. I started visiting from room to room in my white hospital gown, dragging along my stand and IV drip bottle. One elderly lady, when I walked into her room, immediately asked, "Are you an angel?" We had a good visit. I don't know if she crossed over or left the hospital, but she was gone the following day.

The doctors said I made a remarkable recovery and sent me home after about five days. Soon after arriving home, I began having a hard time breathing. I started struggling for breath and then collapsed. An ambulance was called, and I went back in the hospital. This time it was for congestive heart failure. Water from my kidneys had backed up into my lungs and into my heart, causing serious complications.

I found myself back in the same hospital ward with my friends, only this time I was too exhausted to do much visiting. It took me almost a year to regain my strength, but ever since then I have felt the overwhelming need to share my experience. Strength permitting, I have done my best to use my influence and my story for encouraging and lifting up those in need.

As I write this book, it has been approximately nine years since I had the kidney failure and congestive heart failure. Since that time I have talked to a lot of people about my experience. Sometimes I speak to small groups of just a few, and occasionally to large groups of several hundred, and often to individuals I just happen to meet. I don't believe much in coincidences and chance meetings any more. I know that most everything that happens to us, and most everyone we meet, is for a purpose, though we often do not understand it at the time.

People often ask me what my life is like now. Simply put, my life has continued to be filled with new and old challenges. I am still legally blind and still have serious kidney problems. Diabetes continually presents an ongoing array of difficulties to wrestle with. I feel that these continuing trials and experiences will help me learn things that will be of use to someone I will meet someday.

About eight years ago I was impressed with the feeling that I should write my experience down so that I could share it with still many others that I may never have the chance to meet personally. This book is the final result of that effort, and I hope it will be of some benefit to those who take time to read it. Hopefully it will make a positive difference in the lives of many.

CHAPTER 6

LESSONS I LEARNED IN THE SPIRIT WORLD

The desire to share the important concepts I learned while standing on the hill is very strong. The information was so extensive that it would be impossible to write it all down. My understanding at that time was not limited to one item followed by another like here on earth. Instead, I could ask hundreds of questions and receive all of the answers at once and assimilate everything perfectly.

Though the main learning session lasted only a short time, it included some of life's most important questions. Knowledge was gained throughout my visit there, but it is difficult for a person such as myself who has had this type of near-death experience to find earthly words to describe this remarkable world. It would be like taking a person out of the early nineteenth century and sending them into the future where we have satellites, telephones, and microwaves. I'll try to use earthly scenes and objects to describe things I have no words for.

THE IMPORTANCE OF LOVE

I believe that the most important concept I learned while standing upon the hill was just how very much we are loved and the importance of loving and caring for each other in our individual lives. My entire experience was permeated with a feeling of the importance of love. I sensed that everything that Heavenly Father and Jesus Christ do for us is based upon this love that they have for us. It is a very specific love and concern that surpasses every other emotion that we have experienced or can imagine.

They know each and every one of us personally and individually—much better than we know ourselves. They understand our faults and weaknesses, but they also know our strengths and the wonderful things that we are capable of. Although they are aware of the mistakes we make as a part of this human experience, they love us all and sincerely want the very best for each one of us.

One of the main reasons we come to earth is to learn to develop this same kind of pure, unconditional love for others. However, Heavenly Father and Jesus are bound by heavenly laws that define and limit what they can do for us. These laws or rules are ones that they know when followed result in the very best for all concerned, and so they follow them explicitly.

In order for them to bless us, we must comply with these laws here on earth as well as in the spirit world. It is also important to understand that some things that seem like blessings in this mortal life are not really as they appear. In mortality we can obtain wealth and ease through doing evil; but it will only be temporary, and the consequences of doing evil will be severe.

After my NDE, I began reading the New Testament daily. I really had never read the Bible before but now had a strong desire to do so. I read where it talks about charity being more important than anything—more important than prophesying or speaking in tongues or a host of other things. I also read about the importance of loving our neighbors the way we would have them love us. Often we confuse this love with a romantic kind of love, but God's love is very different from that. Charity is the pure love of Christ.

When I stood on the hill and watched as Jesus entered the city, I was able to feel for a small moment the intense love that He has for me and for each of us. It was so intense in fact that it was almost consuming. My most heartfelt desire is to return to the spirit world so that I can once again bask in His love. The next time, however, I want to be able to be worthy to go down into the city and be in His presence.

WE ARE ALL BEAUTIFUL

While on earth we have many things confused as to their relative importance. One idea that we have misplaced is the importance of physical beauty. All people are beautiful, unique, and special no matter what they look like or what clothing they may use to cover themselves. Years earlier I had become involved with the Hollywood scene, which is based largely on physical beauty, fine apparel, perfect faces and bodies, youth, and money.

Those values held dear in the entertainment world are in direct opposition to things as they "really" are. Earth life is temporary. If a beautiful actress were to be horribly scarred in an accident, would she still be beautiful? Here on earth the answer would be no. But in the world beyond that is not the case. The true beauty of our souls and what we have become will go on with us forever.

We spent thousands of years as spirits before coming to earth, and we will spend millions more in the spirit world and beyond after we leave this existence. We are only here on earth for a relatively short span, which seems like a few minutes to everyone in the spirit world. Spending so much of our lives focusing and concentrating all of our efforts on things like the attainment of wealth, beauty, and material possessions is an unbelievable waste of time. Our probation on earth is a time of teaching, learning, overcoming, improving, and preparing for what follows.

THE IMPORTANCE OF HELPING OTHERS

In this growing process called life we can't, and we're not intended to, "go it alone." Nor were we intended to go through these experiences just to benefit ourselves. We are here to travel this life together, learning and growing from each other and thereby succeeding together in the end. We are all connected to and have known each other in a very real way for eons. The person we bump into on the street may have been our best friend before coming to this earth.

Without exception, all of those living upon the earth at the present time knew and loved each other before being born. We don't remember this because shortly after we are born, a block is put on a part of our "spiritual DNA" to prevent us from remembering our lives before coming to earth. However, every once in a while some small memory will leak through the block, and we will have a vague recognition of people or places. That is why many of us may have at some time in our lives met someone that we immediately "clicked" with, someone that we felt we had known "forever." Indeed it may be so.

This reality is one of the reasons I feel so sad when I read about the terrible killings and wars, especially between the Arabs and the Jews. But it is the same for anyone else. They, in their forgetful ignorance, could quite possibly be killing their friends, people they dearly loved before coming to this life. This is another reason why the life review and complete remembering that we experience when we get to the other side is so difficult and painful. At that time, with our memory restored, we will realize the pain we inflicted was upon our brothers and sisters, our friends from long ago.

Another truth is that we cannot go to Heaven alone. If a major part of this life's existence is to learn to help and love others, then we cannot live like hermits and expect to go to heaven. I once read that Mother Theresa said, "Love is service to others." I think that is it exactly. It is by serving others, helping them to become better people and loving them, that we learn the true principle of love. We grow and progress by doing for and giving to others in need, as Mother Theresa said, by service.

I recently heard a story about a young man who performed a simple act of service that saved someone's life. A boy who was considered a "geek" at school dropped a large pile of books while on his way home from school. Another young man, who was one of the most popular boys at school, was right there and asked if he needed help and then helped the "geek" to his feet and picked up all of the spilled books. They gradually became friends.

Years later, the boy who had fallen down and dropped his books was giving a lecture and divulged that when this incident took place back in high school, he was about to do something drastic. He had been so completely discouraged that he had cleaned out his locker so that no one would have to deal with the mess, and then he planned to commit suicide later that day. The kindly lift he was given in his time of need turned him around in his thoughts and stopped him from acting out his intention. We do not realize how many times simple acts of kindness, a reassuring word, or a smile can give another courage to go on.

XOI-COI

I also learned a word that is used in the spirit world for which an equivalent in our language does not exist. The word is xoi-coi. Though I'm not sure of the spelling, it is pronounced "x-oy koy." This word means "someone who doesn't do anything meaningful while on earth." This person doesn't progress, help others, or care. In a way, he or she just takes up space, doing nothing worthwhile. Unfortunately, I learned there are a lot of spirits who come to earth and become xoi-cois. They live to "party" and spend countless hours trying only to entertain themselves and satisfy their wants, which they will never fill because these pleasures are empty and have no lasting or eternal value. They do nothing to elevate mankind or contribute to the improvement of the world. Such positive contributions may be large or small because all do not have the same power to make a difference, but the important thing is to try. Even very small acts of kindness can make a big difference. I believe that many souls in the world to come will thank us for what we assumed was unappreciated or insignificant.

WHY DO GOOD PEOPLE SUFFER?

One of the questions I asked while on the hill was, "Why did I have to suffer so much pain during my life, especially at the hands of my father?" The reply was that nothing any of us suffer in this life would be more than we could stand, and that in every hardship a way is provided to deal with it or to overcome it. Our lives on earth, the things that we experience of good and bad, are designed especially to help us grow and are all part of a great plan for us.

As God plans and prepares blessings for us, I learned that there is an evil spirit we call Satan who, with the assistance of other spirits like him, orchestrates bad experiences in our lives. Satan, I learned, is a very real spirit person. He was the leader of a group of spirits who rebelled or tried to fight against God a long time ago before we came to earth. I cannot begin to express how evil these spirits are. No mayhem, debauchery, destruction, or wickedness exists that Satan and his cospirits will not do or persuade people to do.

It is these evil spirits who cause or instigate most of the terrible things that happen here on earth. While God and Christ are always in complete control, they do temporarily allow Satan and his evil spirits a certain amount of freedom to influence people for bad and to attempt to draw people away from the right path. In this way God and Jesus allow us to be tested to

There Is No Death

see which way we will choose to go and whom we will follow. They allow those who permit themselves to be influenced by evil ones to commit crimes against the innocent as a testament against them and their works.

God also allows unpleasant things to happen to us because of the growth, understanding, and strength we will gain. For example, without misery there would be no compassion. Without pain we would not appreciate well-being. God does not interfere with our individual agency to choose good or evil. He does not "cause" bad things to happen to us but allows us to learn our greatest abilities and strengths through adversity. I learned that it is very important for us to understand pain and suffering and that this was one of the reasons we came to earth. I know that as spirits, before coming to earth, we didn't understand physical pain.

It is also important to know that we are not alone in our pain or suffering. When we hurt, God and Jesus know what it is like and can feel our pain and help us through it. This is because spirit persons can feel the pain or joy of other spirits. In a way that I do not completely understand, this is all necessary to provide the balance needed in this life. This needed balance is different on earth than in Heaven or the spirit world, but it all works together for our good. There is purpose in everything for learning and developing, especially learning compassion and love.

The evil spirits have an advantage that we do not. Their memories have not been blocked the way ours have, and so they remember the thousands of years we lived together where they knew us very well. They know our weaknesses and try to use them to persuade us to make bad choices. They are in torment and suffering because of their evil actions and rebellion against God and are working to make us as miserable as they are.

100

Evil spirits can have power over many mortal, physical things. However, they are limited in what they are permitted to do. God's power is always greater than all powers of evil. For the most part, these spirits work by suggesting things to our minds. Not being able to see these spirits as they do their evil works makes it very difficult to fight back. Once they have succeeded in getting someone to listen to them, they can influence individuals to commit terrible acts, often against good people, thereby causing as much pain, suffering, and misery as they can. The way we can combat this process is to learn to choose right. God will always influence us to choose the right, and as we pray and do what we know is right, we are strengthened against evil.

There are many evil spirits here on the earth. They are all around us and have the ability to roam where they will in this world. Again, they can't really harm us unless we give them power to do so by making bad choices. Often we can feel the presence or influence of these evil spirits. Their primary attitude is one of hate, anger, or depression; and so if we let ourselves go and become uncontrollably angry or hateful we can be fairly sure of their presence and attempts to influence us for bad. Many of the depressed people on the earth today are under the influence of Satan and his evil spirits. Their desire is to cause us to feel downhearted and despondent and to believe that our situation is completely hopeless and beyond our power to change or control. When we are like that, it is much easier for them to influence us to make bad choices.

To counter the influence of those evil spirits, there are also a lot of good spirits around us who whisper to our minds warnings of danger of a physical or spiritual nature and encourage us to make good, positive choices. Usually these good spirits around us are loved ones, family members who have either passed away or who have not yet come to earth. They love us and are constantly looking after us, often speaking peace and hope to our hearts. One of the ways these good spirits communicate with us is through dreams. Deceased loved ones may visit us in dreams and bring feelings of comfort and encouragement. Occasionally when we wake up we can remember specific messages or images, but usually it is just impressions and feelings.

Unfortunately, evil spirits can also use dreams as a means of communication. Most nightmares are actually caused or influenced by evil spirits, often using the bad things we have seen or read to attack us. For this reason it is extremely important to pray at night and ask God to keep us safe from evil. If we fail to ask Him for His protection or help it may not be there for us, as God will not force anything upon us. Force comes from Satan, while God invites and encourages us to choose Him. Some of the good spirits have had special powers given to them to control the evil spirits so they cannot go beyond their bounds. Good spirits also protect us from crossing over before our time. We call these spirits guardian angels.

I once heard of a group of children in Wyoming who were taken hostage in a school by a madman. The man had a bomb with him that went off, killing him and his companion, but all of the children miraculously escaped. Several of the children later told stories of people dressed in white who had appeared to them and told them where to stand and what to do, preparing them for the explosion. Later some of the children actually identified deceased relatives from photographs as the people who helped them in their time of need. This is just one of the examples of how help can come from the other side. There have been questions about angels attending those who suffered in the 9-11 attacks on the World Trade Center. I am sure this happened and that angels, including departed loved ones, were with them during the ordeal and as they crossed over. I can truly see angels holding hands with many who leaped from those tall buildings.

We are always given a choice between good and evil. As I said earlier, it is a law that has to be obeyed here. That is why evil will have its opportunity to become very powerful in the near future. However, God is in complete control, and we must trust Him. It is all part of the balance.

God often works in very different ways than what we may think he should. As an example, I like to think of Moses in Egypt. To our mortal minds, it would have been so simple for God to have allowed Moses to become the next Pharaoh, ruler of all Egypt. That way Moses could have easily released the children of Israel from slavery. However, instead of the simple way, God set up a confrontation between Moses and an evil Pharaoh. It was a tremendous battle between good and evil, with plagues and destruction. God accomplished his will in this way so that the people would see the difference between God's way, that of good, and Satan's evil way, as shown through Pharaoh. The people learned to trust God and to follow His prophet. Even with the many miracles they saw, however, the children of Israel still had a difficult time being obedient.

THE IMPORTANCE OF FORGIVENESS

Another very important lesson I learned, mostly when I visited my father in spirit prison, was the importance of forgiveness. Forgiveness is essential. The people in Hell will not be able to leave that terrible place and progress until the people they have wronged forgive them. It is not enough that they suffer the pain of the hurt they inflicted upon others or have a change in their hearts so they no longer desire to hurt others. They must receive the forgiveness of the people they have injured.

We need to also understand the responsibility that we have in the forgiveness process. There is a connection between people who have hurt others and those who have been hurt. The way to break that connection is for the injured person to forgive. We must forgive those who have injured us emotionally or physically to free ourselves from that connection and to make ourselves acceptable to the Lord. Without forgiveness, both the person who inflicted the pain and the person who received it will be bound, dragged down in a spiritual sense, and unable to progress. We ourselves in this sense are responsible for damning our own progress and halting our opportunity to move forward. Also, when we forgive, the Lord blesses us in special ways.

DÉJÀ VU

As I mentioned previously, I learned that before we came to earth, we lived as spirits. We lived together for a very long time and learned and grew in that environment. I am not sure of all that we learned, but I know that love, kindness, and concern for others were taught. Self-control was another of the important concepts that we tried to learn before we came to the earth.

When it came time for us to come here, we were given the choice, once again, as to whether we wanted to live as mortals for a time on earth or to remain in God's presence. No one was ever forced to do anything. It was all a matter of agency.

After our choice was made to become mortal, we formed groups and were organized with those spirits we wanted to have as part of our earthly family. Usually we chose to be with those spirits to whom we were closest, the spirit friends we loved the most and from whom we could learn the most.

As we made this choice, we were shown some of what our life on earth would be like. We were given small glimpses into our future life. God could somehow look into the future and show some of the things that would happen to us. He was able, to a great degree, to show us some of the joys, some of the suffering, and some of the challenges we would face. Even with that we were still excited for the opportunity to come to earth and experience mortality.

Our circumstances differ with the families we come into, the time when we are born, and so on. All this was measured for our good. All of us chose to come to earth because we knew the experience as mortals was the plan of God for His children to achieve their greatest potential, with the possibility to eventually become more like Him and Jesus. God showed us some of the bad and unhappy circumstances so that our decision to be born would be a choice based on complete understanding of what lay ahead.

I understood that I had been shown how difficult this journey would be, and I had chosen to come anyway. As a spirit I understood that the greater the trials were, the greater the growth and learning would be. Terrible problems looked like exciting challenges that we would surely be able to overcome. Of course the actual experiences here on earth seem much harder than they looked on our "preview screen." Seeing a movie where someone is hurt or in pain is very different from actually feeling the pain ourselves.

105

Déja vu is simply our fragmented memories of those preview scenes that were shown to us. This is why we sometimes know exactly what someone is going to say, or we have the sense that we have been in this same place before— because we have seen it before.

REINCARNATION

Reincarnation also has to do with the life we had before we came to earth and the fact that everything we experience is recorded in our "spiritual DNA." I have often used the term spiritual DNA as a label for how and where it is recorded in our spirit-selves because I do not know how else to describe this remarkable process of complete retention of information.

As I have mentioned, before we came to earth we had formed close relationships, friendships with each other as spirits. We wanted to continue our friendships and come to earth at the same time so we could experience life together. Occasionally, however, this was not always possible, and a loved one came to earth ahead of us. When this happened, we could at times receive permission to accompany them to earth as a guardian angel. In this way we were able to be with them and assist them throughout their lives. We could also then closely observe the experiences of their mortal lives and gain a better idea of what earth life would be like for us in the future.

I have an example that I use often to help explain how this works. Suppose one of my very closest friends in the spirit world came to earth a hundred years before I did, and I received permission to come and be one of her guardian angels. I was constantly by her side, heard what she heard, witnessed her experiences, and felt what she felt. In a way I was living her life with her. I was present at her birth and saw her as a little girl when she fell out of a tree and broke her arm. I was there with her when she married her sweetheart and watched with her as he went off to the Civil War. I was by her side as she nursed him back to health after he had been wounded and watched with love and compassion as years later she buried him and a baby at the same time.

A hundred years later I am living on the earth having my own experiences and by coincidence one day I am drawn to visit a house in the South, the very house that my dear friend lived in. The house seems familiar and I can tell bits and pieces about the lady who lived in the house. I am able to tell about her birth, family, husband, and events of her life. I can tell so much that I have the feeling that I might have actually been her, and that I had lived before, and now have been reincarnated in my present life. In actuality, I am only remembering my friend's life events because I had been by her side experiencing them as a spirit. We only get one chance at living in mortality.

Again, there is no such thing as reincarnation. It is the simple remembrance of shared experiences of someone else's life that have been recorded on our spiritual DNA.

INSECTS AND ANIMALS

I did not see any insects in the spirit world. It was my understanding that when they cross over they go to an entirely different place prepared just for them—a lower world, sort of a spirit world for insects. Most of the animals are the same. They also go to a place where they can be happy and be with their own kind. The exceptions are those animals that would be happiest living with a person who loves them. We will be able to enjoy the company of our pets that we loved and had stewardship over while we were on the earth.

PEOPLE WHO ARE MURDERED

I asked a question about people who are murdered and experience so much terrible pain when they die. I wondered what happened to those who suffer before they die? The answer was comforting. Often, especially in the case of children, the spirit leaves the body before much of the pain occurs so that they do not feel it. Somehow, with his infinite love, God has made provisions so that the body will still appear alive, but the person or spirit does not inhabit it any longer and is cut off from experiencing much of the torment and pain. Those individuals who participate in the shedding of innocent blood will forever suffer a torment far worse than their victim ever did.

THE MENTALLY HANDICAPPED

I learned that those people who are born mentally handicapped, like children with Downs Syndrome, knew that they were going to be born with that challenge and chose to come anyway. Children born with those challenges are very special spirits, already full of tremendous love. They are some of the very best and most noble of God's children. They come to earth primarily to receive a body and help others learn how to love and give service. In reality, it is a great blessing to have one of these children born into your home if they are welcomed and cared for with love and gratitude. They do not have to be tried and tested in ways that we do and are already received into Heavenly Father's highest kingdom.

OTHER ABILITIES OF SPIRIT BODIES

I became aware of many abilities of the spirit body. Spirit bodies have the ability to travel into the past and actually see, hear, and experience things that have already happened. They do not, however, have the power to change or influence outcomes. They are merely in a position of observation. I found that there are many dimensions, and spirits can easily travel between them. The future is in another dimension, and occasionally spirits are permitted to travel there. Spirits are also able to travel to different worlds and planets if they desire, and it all happens at the speed of a thought. I was impressed that the spirit world is actually occupying the same space as the earth but in a different dimension. That is why departed family members know much of what is going on in our lives and are concerned with our progress or lack thereof. In reality, they are very near to us. If the "film" were removed from our eyes, we would see them all around us.

LIFE ON OTHER PLANETS

I have been asked several times if I had any information about life on planets other than earth. The answer is that there are many planets in the universe that are inhabited with beings just like us, because they also are made in the image of God, but we need not be concerned with what is going on elsewhere. They are not a threat to us as many suppose, though it is possible that some of them might visit us. Grotesque beings from other worlds that supposedly visit this earth and are seen by humans are actually evil spirits who can take on whatever form they wish to in order to confuse and deceive.

There Is No Death

MUSIC, DRUGS AND ALCOHOL

Music, as many people are already aware, has a powerful effect directly upon the spirit. Music does have power of influence for good or evil in varying degrees, a kind of spirit of its own. It can encourage us to be better people and motivate us to help others, or it can do just the opposite and stimulate us to do evil and turn away from God. Evil music consisting of sexual lyrics or violent suggestions can and does attract evil spirits and in a way gives them more power over us so that we can be influenced easily to do acts of evil. When I became so depressed that I committed suicide, I played music over and over again that had a negative effect upon me and helped surround me with destructive spirits. The music weakened my spiritual stamina, so to speak, and gave the evil around me greater power. I gave in to the depression and listened to their whisperings.

The use of prayer, good music, uplifting books, and so forth, can increase our resistance to evil spirits and actually drive them away.

Drugs and alcohol are some of the most powerful tools of the evil ones. One of the goals of evil spirits is to take control of our bodies, since they have none of their own. This allows them to really feel the senses, pleasures, and pain that otherwise they cannot.

Before a spirit comes to earth, it cannot feel sensation. Once a spirit has been joined to a physical, mortal body, its senses are much stronger. After death, when the body goes back to being dust and the spirit crosses over, the spirit can feel the senses much better than before it came to earth. However, it still misses the

110

physical part of the body. I came to understand that later on the spirit and a new, glorious body will be joined together. This process is called the resurrection and happens after a period of time in the spirit world. It is at this point that a person is assigned to one of the kingdoms of glory that lie beyond this temporary world.

When an evil spirit enters a human physical body, we call it a "possession." It happens much more frequently than we realize. Possessions can be very mild or extend to complete control. All of us have a natural resistance to such a possession so that evil spirits cannot enter into us. However, when we partake of mind-altering drugs and alcohol, this resistance is lowered. It can happen with the first drink. A hole opens up at the crown of the head that actually allows an evil spirit to drop down into us. Once inside, they have a greater power over us and can influence our behavior to a great degree. This is why Satan and his evil cohorts encourage the use of alcohol and drugs. It is also why so many heinous crimes are committed under the influence of these substances. We will be held responsible for the acts we commit while under their influence. We should never take them into our bodies and should be careful of our association with those who are controlled by these mind-altering tools. A hard truth is that Satan often works through so called "friends" to pull us down.

Many people are under the false impression that occasional recreational drug use does not hurt anyone else. In reality hundreds of innocent lives are lost yearly from drug trafficking. Drug enforcement officers and others are murdered for their continued efforts to fight the losing battle against drugs in our country. If the demand for these harmful substances were to cease then so would all of the evil activities associated with them.

111

Every time an individual buys or uses an illegal drug, somewhere in the world people's lives are being taken to provide it for them. In some way the "user" and the "seller" are responsible in some measure for the deaths of those souls. There is nothing innocent or harmless in the use of marijuana, misused prescription drugs, or any illegal substances.

SPIRITUALISM, WITCHCRAFT, AND SORCERY

Along with the understanding about evil spirits and how they had been involved in influencing my suicide (empowered by many of the poor choices I had made), I understood that there are people on earth who encourage and help evil spirits turn others away from God and commit evil acts. Spiritualism, witchcraft, sorcery, Ouija boards, and so on, are all ways that encourage and assist evil spirits. People who engage in these types of behaviors are easily influenced by these sources and may be led to believe they are talking to a loved one. The Lord has always warned people to stay clear of psychics and mediums for these reasons.

People who "channel" spirits are always taken over or possessed by the wrong kind of spirits, often pretending to be someone's dearly departed relative or friend. They can do this easily because they have seen our lives and know what has happened and what to say to convince unsuspecting victims. Those evil spirits also enjoy pretending to be higher beings or aliens from other worlds. They will do anything to get people to listen to and believe them. They are willing to tell many truths to lure people away from God and believe in them, slipping in the one lie that will clinch their control at the most vulnerable, critical moment. Those on the other side who need to know and have power to help us are already aware of our thoughts and feelings and hopes and fears and do not need to be "summoned" up for any reason.

GOOD WINS IN THE END
BECAUSE GOD IS IN CONTROL

Though we will very soon go through some terrible times, good will eventually triumph over evil. Evil must have its "day." It has something to do with the balance that must exist here on earth. Though it may not seem so at all times in today's world, God is always in control.

Jesus Christ will return to the earth and reward the good people with tremendous blessings, including his presence, once again. It will be a wonderful time, very similar to what it is like in the paradise part of the spirit world. During this time, evil will not be able to have any effect upon us. Through some process, the evil spirits will not be able to influence those who remain. This wonderful time of peace and happiness is not very far off, and I believe that many of us now living will make it through the bad times that lie ahead to experience the joyous times that follow. The Lord will have a remnant of people left to greet Him and help to build up and establish His kingdom. Others who survive will be so sick of death, hate, and war that they will finally be ready to learn God's ways. God, our Father, wants all of His children to make it back to Him having had a successful journey. Those who do not reject His message of love and helping others will have that successful journey.

CHAPTER 7

COMMONLY ASKED QUESTIONS AND ANSWERS

The following questions and replies are taken from transcripts of several different presentations that Sarah has made over the last five years. They have been modified slightly to fit a written format. Though in no specific order, they are listed as Q1, Q2, and so forth. Occasionally there are follow-up questions as well. In that case they are listed as Q1a and Q1b.

Q1a: YOU SAY BAD THINGS THAT HAPPEN TO US ARE REALLY FOR OUR GOOD AND ALMOST NOTHING HAPPENS BY ACCIDENT?

Almost everything that happens to us in our lives, including every person that we meet, is part of a plan for each one of us. Very little of it is by accident. Our lives and the surrounding circumstances are all part of a huge plan that we are a part of. What we do and how we react when those trials happen is up to us, and so the choices we make have a great deal to do with it as well. But there are forces working hard to arrange circumstances for us and then influence our decisions in responding to them. Both good and evil spirits pull strings in our lives to make events happen. Do you think you could travel down all of these paths throughout your life and by coincidence run into just the right person at just the right time, in just the right place, without some help? God arranges things so everything that happens to us can work for our benefit, if we allow it to.

The trials of my life have allowed me to help hundreds of people who are going through similar experiences. I do not ever look at any hardship in my life and think of it as horrible anymore. The Lord does not give us these experiences as punishments or even necessarily as trials. We suffer the natural consequences of our actions. However, the Lord orchestrates the outcome for our benefit and learning, allowing us an opportunity to overcome adversity.

Q1b: SO YOU ARE SAYING THAT GOD DOESN'T CAUSE BAD THINGS AS A TEST FOR US? HE DID NOT CAUSE HITLER TO KILL PEOPLE?

No, God did not cause those terrible things to happen. God does not work that way. However, certain things are allowed to happen, often things that come as a natural consequence to something we have done or some choice we have made. Sometimes we put ourselves into situations that have a negative effect on us. However, many times people suffer because of the evil acts and choices of others. God seldom interferes with the agency of bad people.

Before I attempted suicide I could not believe there was a God or anyone in Heaven that could love me and still allow me to go through the trials I had gone through. Now I look at it just the other way around. I can talk to people who are ill, in despair or sorrow, or who have broken marriages, and I can feel sympathy for them in their situation and say something that will lift or elevate that person. I know that if I had not had those experiences I not only would not have had understanding, I would not have had the words to speak to them.

Now I look at some events that have happened recently in my life that have really hurt me. I have shed plenty of tears and prayed probably more than I have in my entire life for someone I love very much, and yet I know that there is a purpose in what I am going through, and I continue to learn from these "unfriendly experiences." I know that the Savior is in total control, even at this trying time in my life.

Q2: IF THERE ARE NO INSECTS IN THE SPIRIT WORLD, WHY DO WE HAVE THEM HERE?

They are here because insects give balance to nature. They serve a purpose in the form of plagues and in pestering mankind. A balance is established in mortal nature that is not had or needed in the spirit world because it is not necessary there. Insects also have intelligence, but they are creatures of a lower intelligence, serving a lower purpose.

Q3a: DID YOU SEE OR LEARN ANYTHING WITH REGARD TO THE MARK OF THE BEAST OR THE EVIL KINGDOM THAT IS TALKED ABOUT IN THE BIBLE?

There is an evil kingdom here on earth that is directed by Satan. There are people on earth who serve him, just like there are people who serve God and Jesus. Many people knowingly serve Satan while others serve his purposes without understanding how they are doing so.

Most of the work of this evil kingdom is done in secret, in darkness, by people who plot to force everyone in the world to serve them and their master. The adversary's armies, born and unborn, are all over the world working toward this goal. They have been at it for a long time and are getting close to success. There are so many who are now serving Satan instead of God. Their goal is to have a time when darkness, chaos, terror, and evil will reign supreme, when most or all of the world would serve Satan instead of God. God and Jesus will allow this to happen for a short period of time so that we can show where our hearts lie.

Q3b: EXPLAIN WHAT YOU MEAN BY THIS SATANIC GOAL OF WORLD CONQUEST.

The whole plan has been plotted out by this secret society of Satan's followers as they have listened to his whisperings. These armies of evil people who are on this earth have for some time plotted towards a one-world government and a one-world religion, including the mark of the beast that will force everyone away from God so they will serve Satan instead. Only a very few people will refuse to do this.

Most people believe that there will be some sort of literal mark of the beast—the implant or chip in the hand or on the forehead. This I believe is true, though I did not see it. But besides the physical mark, I think what people are going to come to realize is that many already are a part of Babylon and have the spiritual mark of the beast upon them. I think the spiritual mark in the hand represents selfishness and greed as we reach out and take everything that the world has to offer. This is done in various ways, both overtly and subtly.

I believe the mark of the beast in the forehead, in a spiritual way, is thinking in the ways of Babylon: wanting more possessions or becoming vane and selfish. It does not mean you must have a chip put in your forehead in order for the prophecy to be fulfilled. For most of us, the spiritual part of it has already come to pass. We are already part of Babylon and the mark of the beast when we get more credit cards and go into more debt for selfish, unnecessary reasons. We want, we want, we want more. We want the most expensive car. We want a huge house. Our thoughts and intents are on the more. It is all for self-gratification and a self-centered attitude, which is just the opposite of what we should be doing by using our means to help others.

People serve Satan's kingdom, the kingdom of the beast, by acts of sex outside of marriage; by drug use which supports a culture that promotes prostitution, murder, thievery, pornography, lying, rape, and every other evil practice; by alcohol use which often supports a similar list of ugliness; by women wearing revealing clothes, or hardly any clothes at all—the same type of fashion that follows the pattern that Satan has used to destroy morality since the time of Adam; and in many other ways. Sodom and Gomorrah are the best-known examples of this process, but I learned that every time a society has been destroyed, the same "fashion of undress" can be found.

Many people assume that sexual sin outside of marriage is the act of complete intercourse. However, any form of sexual

119

pleasure or the touching in any way of another's personal and private parts of their body are actions forbidden by God. Only in the sacred bonds of marriage should such feelings be expressed. Evil leaders and men who are "of the world" will tell the people that other forms of sexual practice are not really sex. This is an abominable lie and will drag many souls into a web of sorrow and deception.

We serve Satan by having and supporting abortion, which is a selfish, Satan-inspired act that destroys the sacred role of motherhood. We also serve Satan by producing and listening to vulgar and violent music and by watching sexual or violent movies. These are in a way recruiting tools of Satan, and people who listen to and watch them invite evil spirits into their lives and give these evil spirits power over themselves. What we take into our minds we take into our hearts. All these things aid Satan's goal of world conquest.

Q4: DO WE AS SPIRITS EVER GET TO COME BACK TO EARTH AFTER WE DIE?

Yes, we do. For example, everyone is allowed to come back for his or her own funeral. People can come back for special occasions, like seeing their son or daughter getting married or some other important event. It would be possible to be assigned as a guardian angel for a relative and therefore spend a lot of time with them on earth. But good people who cross over are busy doing important work in the spirit world and do not have time to waste without purpose.

I understand that when our loved ones who have crossed over visit us, it is most often in our dreams during our "alpha awareness state" when we are more easily susceptible to spiritual communication. They whisper and tell us things, encourage us, and give us ideas during this time. Unfortunately this works both ways, and evil spirits also try to use this sleep state. When they do, they often cause terrible nightmares. The "Little Child's Prayer" is not just meant for children. It should be part of our prayers every night as well. We should ask Heavenly Father to watch over us and keep our souls safe. I learned that there is real power in prayer, and God hears every one of them that is sincere, though often He answers them in His own time and in ways we do not expect.

Q5: ARE THERE SUCH THINGS AS GHOSTS?

Yes, there are. Sometimes a person dies, and they do not realize it. I didn't for a while, even while I was looking at my body. Some refuse to recognize that they have died. They are free to wander as spirits as long as they want to, perhaps visiting places where they used to live. But most of the time, especially if the person has been good on earth, they are met by a loved one and guided to some place in the spirit world. Mischievous spirits are the ones that haunt houses, knock things over, and make noises. Righteous spirits are not involved in such practices.

Q6: WHY DO SOME PEOPLE HAVE SO MANY TALENTS WHILE OTHERS HAVE SO FEW?

It has a lot to do with what they did during their life before coming to earth and a little concerning what trials they will undergo here in mortal life. A person can also develop new talents if they have the desire to search out and discover

121

them. Those with great gifts or talents may have tremendous trials and difficulties to overcome. Talents in the areas of music, painting, athletics, intelligence, wisdom, charisma, and leadership are some of these gifts. Their biggest test will be to see how they use their great talents. Will they use them to help elevate others, or will they use them for selfishness and the destruction of others?

It is usually very easy to pick out these great spirits. A few of them are George Washington, Abraham Lincoln, Ghandi, Martin Luther King, Mother Theresa, and the Dahli Lama. There are other great and noble spirits we have been blessed with more recently. Oprah Winfrey is a choice daughter of our Father in Heaven whom I admire very much. She has had great obstacles to overcome in her life, yet has done a tremendous amount to lift and elevate mankind. She has changed and influenced the lives of millions of our Father's children, especially women, in a positive way.

Others also affect mankind for good, but in different ways. For example, Christopher Reeves and Michael J. Fox learned of the spiritual strength they possessed which was unknown to them and the world until after their terrible tragedies. These men and others like them, by facing their adversities with courage and dignity, give hope to many who suffer. These are just some who are visible to us. There are many others who are quietly valiant and true and good.

Of course there are those who have great notoriety and who have used their fame for evil purposes. Everyone thinks of people like Hitler, Stalin, and Saddam Hussein. But others like the purveyors of pornography—including the popular nude magazines—who have used their talents to destroy people and foster Satan's evil kingdom, are almost as bad. Unfortunately, a majority of talented actors, actresses, and musicians, both male and female, help promote Satan's kingdom by their lewd dress and immoral actions. We accept this form of evil more readily because it comes in the form of entertainment. These people will have to face the responsibility for their actions and pay the penalties.

Q7:   IS THERE A WAY TO AVOID THE TERRIBLE THINGS YOU SAW—THE PLAGUES AND DESTRUCTION?

YES. We can easily avoid everything I saw. Nothing is written in stone. It is actually very simple—come back to God! Keep God's commandments like we used to do. This country was founded on the principle of serving God and His beloved son Jesus Christ and keeping their commandments, which are outlined in the scriptures. As long as the people in this country have kept the commandments, they have been blessed. But when they haven't, they have had problems.

I know that the reason we are going to have these terrible events happen to the people in this country is primarily because the majority of its citizens have forsaken God. They are more interested in making money, having fun, and in pleasing themselves than in helping each other.   They don't mind hurting or cheating others to get ahead. It seems that they do everything they can to forget God and push Him away. When we do that, there are going to be consequences.   God will no longer protect and bless this people or this land.

This allows Satan and his army to have more power. They are turning, and have turned, many people away from

God to do what Satan wants them to do. They have wanted to take control of the people in the world for a long, long time and have been planning and working toward that end from the very beginning. They succeeded during Noah's time, and they are succeeding with most of the people now. I know that a large part of our society is as wicked now as it was during the time of Noah and Sodom and Gomorrah just before they were destroyed. If we want to change what is going to happen, then we need to change our actions and our attitudes. And we need to do it very quickly.

Q8: DID YOU SEE ANYTHING ABOUT THE RAPTURE?

Well, yes and no. I didn't actually see the rapture take place, but I know that it happened after the time of chaos and destruction, but before the final, complete annihilation of the wicked by the huge ball of fire. The people who were in the cities of light were the very ones who would be taken up during the rapture. They were those who continued to keep the commandments of God, who still worshiped Jesus and wouldn't deny Him. I also believe that there will be honorable people from non-Christian religions there. That is why the Holy Spirit protected them and guided them to gather to the cities of light for protection. Those good people were on the earth for most of the chaos and destruction, though they didn't suffer the way the wicked did. I knew that God was protecting them from most of the devastations, but what they had to endure was still very difficult. Then just before the entire earth was consumed and the last of the wicked were destroyed by the huge fireball, the righteous were removed from it.

Q9: HOW SOON DO YOU THINK THESE THINGS WILL HAPPEN AND HOW LONG HAVE YOU TALKED ABOUT THE BUILDINGS FALLING IN NEW YORK?

I have been talking about the buildings falling down in New York for over eight years, ever since I felt I needed to tell my story to more people. Four years ago, I did a four-hour interview with a local TV reporter during which I talked about the buildings falling, though they didn't use that in the broadcast of the interview.

How soon do I think the next event will happen? I think it is very soon. When I saw the World Trade Center towers fall, I knew this was part of what I had seen in my experience. That was the first event. The next thing I understood was that this event would be followed by an economic collapse and then the biological attacks on the major cities.

Obviously, we can see that the country is in a recession now, headed for a depression. I am surprised that the biological attacks haven't happened yet. I expect them at any time, and conditions will get bad very quickly thereafter. It could happen this year, next year, or possibly later. I feel it will be sooner rather than later.

Q10: ARE THERE SOME PLACES THAT ARE SAFER THAN OTHERS?

Well, I moved from Los Angeles and out of California. Los Angeles is going to be hit hard. That area has a lot of bad memories for me anyway, which is a big part of why I moved.

As far as places or states that are generally safer than others, there really aren't any. The entire country of America, and around the world, is going to be affected by what is coming. But I believe North America will be affected the most. I would move away from the coasts and any large city and certainly from volcanic areas, though there will be new volcanoes erupting where there haven't been any.

I saw major devastations take place in New York, Los Angeles, San Francisco, and Salt Lake City. However, most every city will be hit with some devastation. The center of the United States, somewhere near Kansas City and St. Louis, will be particularly hard hit as well, with nuclear bombs and a tremendous earthquake. In my vision the earthquake sunk all of the land along the Mississippi River from the Great Lakes to the Gulf of Mexico so that it was all under water.

Common sense tells us that if times get bad, such as the electricity being shut down for whatever reason, it would not be wise to be in a big city like Los Angeles, Chicago, New York, or other places like that. I personally would like to have a house out in the country or some place where I could have a garden and be away from the mainstream. Right now I live in a large city, but I am working on moving away to a much smaller town. But even the small towns will eventually be affected by what occurs. The only true safe places were the cities of light that were scattered across the country. When conditions go bad, if we are close enough to the Lord, he will direct us to one of these gathering places.

Q11: HOW CAN WE PREPARE
FOR WHAT IS COMING?

There will be a time, perhaps three or four years long, when there won't be any food at all, no electricity, or anything. For part of the time it will be so dark that it will even be hard to grow any food in a garden. I have been able to put away food and other supplies on a very limited income because I believe that a time will come when my family will need it. I know that if the desire is there, anyone can prepare.

I have run into a lot of people, some religious and some not, who have felt very strongly about putting food and other supplies away, like winter clothing in case of a long-term emergency. Y2K and September 11th helped people realize how fragile our society is and how easily it could be disrupted. The benefit of Y2K was that for the first time a lot of people thought about what would happen if the electricity did go off for a long period of time. I never felt that Y2K would bring about the conditions I saw, but now with recent terrorist attacks, people realize that anything could happen and life as we know it could change overnight.

The four cities I saw hit were exposed with disease that resulted from a biological attack. Our government, and everyone, tells us that this could happen at any time. I know it will happen soon. My advice for people is to get food, water, winter clothing, hiking shoes, and so forth, and the means to protect themselves against the marauding gangs that will go around killing people. It might be good to have like-minded friends who have prepared so that they could all gather together to help protect each other. There will be safety in numbers; however, the best preparation we can make is not with food, water, and other material supplies, though these are vital. The most important preparation is spiritual preparation! Keeping God's commandments is lifesaving. Not enough people in America or in the world really live by these teachings anymore. I believe that is why evil is becoming so powerful, and we are accepting and becoming conditioned by it. We now see society allowing standards that were not acceptable even five years ago.

I learned that special protection will be given to those who faithfully keep the Sabbath day holy. It is a day for worshiping God and serving others and not for sports, entertainment, or work. Being kind to others, forgiving those who hurt you, reading God's word, visiting the sick, and praying are very important too in spiritual preparation. I feel that I can promise that it won't matter if a person has tons of food and a whole army with them. If they are not truly serving God, then they will not be protected.

Q12: DID YOU EVER FIND OUT WHO THE BEAUTIFUL WOMAN WAS THAT YOU SAW?

A few years after my return to mortality, my sister and I had to place our elderly mother into a care facility and were going through some old photographs that I had never seen before. I saw a picture of a woman and asked my sister who she was. She was my grandmother, Sarah, who died when I was a baby. I had never met her. When I saw the photograph, I immediately recognized her as the beautiful lady in the spirit world who sent me back.

Q13: WILL WE LOOK THE SAME IN THE SPIRIT WORLD AS WE DO HERE?

Yes and no. We will be recognizable because our features will generally be the same, similar to what we look like now, only there won't be any flaws. There will be no weight problems, no scars, or any type of physical defect.

Q14: WHY DO YOU THINK YOU HAD THIS EXPERIENCE?

I am not sure why. I don't think of myself as someone special. I am just an ordinary person who had an extraordinary experience. God often uses the simple or meek to do his work. My experience turned my life around, especially concerning the hate and anger for my father that was consuming and destroying me. For approximately the first twelve years after this took place, I thought it was just to help me. I shared it only with a few people, usually one person at a time.

Grandmother Sarah

After I had the kidney problem and congestive heart failure eight years ago and nearly crossed over again, I felt strongly that I needed to share my story with others. I then started speaking to large groups of people. I discovered that many more individuals wanted to hear "the message." The groups continued to grow even larger, and it was difficult to keep up with the demands of answering so many questions. After a friend, Caren, and I saw the movie "Contact," I heard some people sitting behind us saying, "I wonder if there really is life after death?" I felt filled with the Spirit and told my friend that I knew that God wanted me to write a book about my NDE so that it could reach many more people.

I believe the reason that I remember everything that happened is so that I can share the message and perhaps help others who are "lost" in this world and give them hope. I am not a prophetess or a psychic. I am just a simple person who had a remarkable experience. When this happened to me, I was not sure that there was a God. Now I know there is. Without exception when I speak to people, they tell me afterwards that I have answered important questions they have been struggling with or helped change their life in a positive direction. I am beginning to understand that this is the reason for the knowledge I was given. My hope is that I can encourage more people to draw close to their Father in Heaven and have a better understanding of the purpose of life.

Q15: WHAT DOES CHRIST LOOK LIKE?

He is beautiful beyond description. There are really no earthly words to do him justice. His brightness and glory are far beyond the brilliance of the sun. He is the light of the world. His hair appeared to be shoulder length and was a dark golden blonde. His eyes were a piercing blue, almost unreal. He was not thin and weak, but powerful, and yet he encompassed the word love completely. Seeing the Savior finally helped me understand what the word love means. He Is Love.

I hope that everyone who has read this book will come away with the understanding that God does live and loves each one of us. He wants His people who are worthy and prepared to survive the calamities that are ahead of us. I know the Lord will be there to help us do so.

We need to be assured that even at a time when the world seems to be completely out of control the Savior will always be in complete control, and good will triumph over evil. We have no need to fear because the King of our universe will make all wrongs right.

FINAL NOTE:

LEARNING MORE ABOUT THE EVENTS OF THE LAST DAYS AND HOW TO PREPARE FOR THEM

There are many excellent resources to help understand the prophecies and events of the last days and how to prepare for what is coming. Web links and lists of recommended books are available at www.thereisnodeath.com, along with instructions on how to send letters to Sarah or obtain her speaking schedule.